QUILTERS

Playtime

Games with Fabrics

Dianne S. Hire

Located in Paducah, Kentucky, the American Quilter's Society (AQS) is dedicated to promoting the accomplishments of today's quilters. Through its publications and events, AQS strives to honor today's quiltmakers and their work and to inspire future creativity and innovation in quiltmaking.

Editor: Toni Toomey
Book Design: Lynda Smith
Illustrations: Toni Toomey
Cover Design: Michael Buckingham
Photography: Charles R. Lynch
Photos contributed by author: Terry M. Hire

Library of Congress Cataloging-in-Publication Data

Hire, Dianne S.
Quilters Playtime : games with fabrics / by Dianne S. Hire
     p. cm.
   ISBN 1-57432-826-3
1. Quilting--Miscellanea. 2. Quilts--Design. 3. Educational
games.   I. Title.
   TT835.H5334 2004
   746.46'041--dc22

                              2003026368

Additional copies of this book may be ordered from the American Quilter's Society, PO Box 3290, Paducah, KY 42002-3290, or online at www.AQSquilt.com.

Dedication

This dedication is to my family–game players, all. They taught me the delight of playing board games, card games, active games, quiet games, car games–real games and those of the imagination. It is no wonder that now I interpret many of those games into quilts and quilt blocks.

> To Pappa, who winked his way over the years to
>   many-a-win at Rook.
> To Mammy, who tolerated his winks and played along.
> To Lou, Danny, Nell, Ken, and Marge, who adopted the wink.
> To Mom, who wouldn't have any part of the wink.
> To Howard, who always left me with the last card, doffing
>   me "The Old Maid."

This dedication is to friends who have tolerated so many forms of game-playing.

> To Leslie who loves the game as much I as do.
> To Barbara and Milt, Sharon, Bill and Bev, John and
>   Priscilla–all have endured my love of games.
> To Dan, who would just rather not play.

This dedication is to quiltmakers across the country who have played along with me, sewing games at their machines with glee even when the heat melts their chocolate. Without their encouragement, this book would never have happened.

But mostly, this dedication is to Terry, my game partner for life–and that will never be a wink.

Acknowledgments

The author wishes to extend warmest thanks to the people whose assistance and generosity encouraged *Playtime* to be written–

I must record my gratitude to contributors of supplies and play-fabrics– Jamie Arcuri at Free Spirit; Mary Scott at Bold Over Batiks; Shirley and Addy of Pinetree Quiltworks, Ltd.; Carl R. Cottrell of Olfa Products Group; and Tracy Whitlock of Fairfield Processing Corporation.

Thank you, Kathleen Vanden Brink, for sharing your beautiful hands in the photographs.

I would also like to thank Patricia Estabrook of All About Games, who shared her knowledge of real games, and Debbie Mailman and Pat Devroy of South Portland Sewing Center for years of maintaining my workhorse sewing machine.

I am indebted to quiltmakers Peggy Ireland Elliot, Sally K. Field, and Alice Hobbs Parsons, who gave a year of their incredible talent, experience, and insight as they diligently stitched quilts for book examples. A special thank you to Judi H. Bastion, Linda Neustadt, Ellie Pancoe, and Nancy F. Wheelwright, who graciously agreed to play along, just for the fun of it, and also created quilts. To Nancy R. Board who, with obstinate perseverance, pushed and pushed again so I would write this book, and then took on the task of being the first person who ever quilted any of my quilts–five of them to be exact–thanks.

I gratefully acknowledge the many quiltmakers from play-classrooms across the USA who submitted images of their play-quilts–there were so many beautiful quilts that, if all were used, they would have made this book a hefty 100-pound volume.

There are not enough words to say thank you to my dear friend Barbara Daggett, who has seriously collected fabrics, beads, buttons, strings, paper, feathers, and many, many other very unlikely embellishments for my quilts over the last fifteen years. Often, it has been her love of strangely unique things that has given me a nudge to create more and better quilts.

I express my gratitude to AQS editors Marjie Russell, Toni Toomey, and Barbara Smith, and to the president of AQS, Meredith Schroeder, all of whom endorsed and encouraged the playbook's writing as well as coerced a better product from a novice writer. To the designers Lynda Smith and Michael Buckingham, and photographer Charles R. Lynch, a sincere thank you.

One quilt that didn't make the final cut is named IT TOOK A VILLAGE TO RAISE QUADRUPLETS. Truth is, it took a village to raise this book.

To each, to all, a heartfelt thanks.

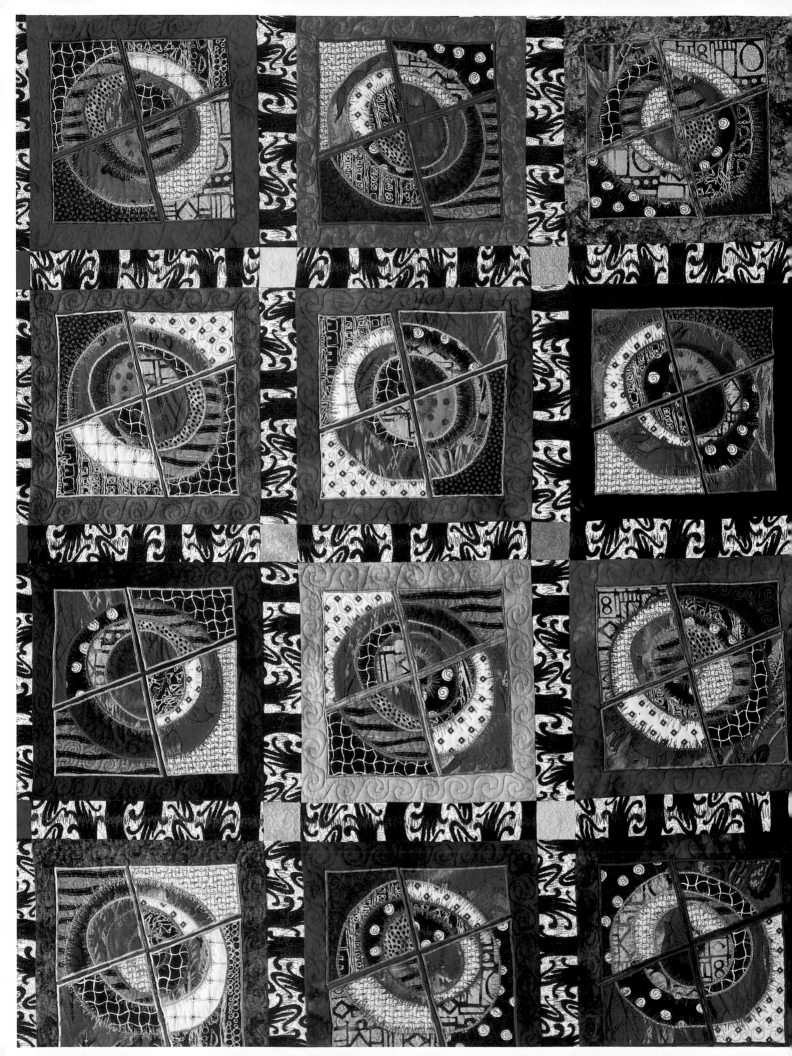

Contents

Foreword

Prepare yourself for a treat. There's a little child inside of you who is already jumping up and down because you are reading a book entitled *Playtime*. For many of us, this little child has been waiting a long time to return to the very early years of life when play was the first and most natural way of behaving. Society wants us to play, play, play in those first few years and then, unfortunately, spends the rest of the time reminding us that we need to grow up and get to work. Here's the rub. What needs to be understood is that play is work in the very best and most constructive sense. Both play and work are serious business. Just think of how much children learn about themselves and life when they are playing. Play is all about being creative, about learning and unlearning, about knowing an experience of joy that never wants to end.

Famous jazz artist Louis Armstrong had the right idea when he said, "What we play is life." He was talking about making music specifically, but for sure, he was also alluding to all other creative experiences as well. Louis loved playing extemporaneously, and at those times, he felt the fullness of life coming out of his soul as well as his horn. For him, playing music and living life was one and the same thing. We can learn from his example. Play is a valuable teacher. Play stretches us to test the edges between reality and fantasy, between linear and oblique ways of thinking. Play finds joy in the process rather than in the product. Play has the potential for discovering order in the madness of a sometimes chaotic world. Play restores our intuitive juices to their rightful dignity, for without intuition, creativity cannot survive. Play becomes a safe environment for experimentation as long as we can shed our fears about it being a waste of time and energy.

Dianne Hire knows how to behave like a child. The little one inside is a very happy girl indeed. In *Playtime*, Dianne shares with us her return journey to the playful little girl inside her creative spirit. Dianne believes that we are limited only by our imaginations, and that our imaginations exist without boundaries. *Playtime* invites you to play games with fabric and thread; to take leaps of faith into unfamiliar places packed with dozens of new and refreshing creative experiences. The resulting journey is one in which deviations from the rules and encounters with unexpected outcomes become the norm. Dianne guides us onto similar paths at the start of each game, but if we play the game right, we will all end up in different places. The best teachers realize that what students need most is a good jump-start. The rest of the journey is theirs to discover as they choose.

So now it's time to get started. It's time to recapture those early childhood experiences of playtime, a time in which play again becomes a tool for unleashing our hidden creative energies— creative energies that have been longing to once again hear the words, "Can _____ come out and play?" You must fill in the blank yourself. It's your decision. Go ahead and fill it in now. There's a playful child waiting to be invited back into your creative life.

David Walker
Artist-Teacher-Quiltmaker
Cincinnati, Ohio

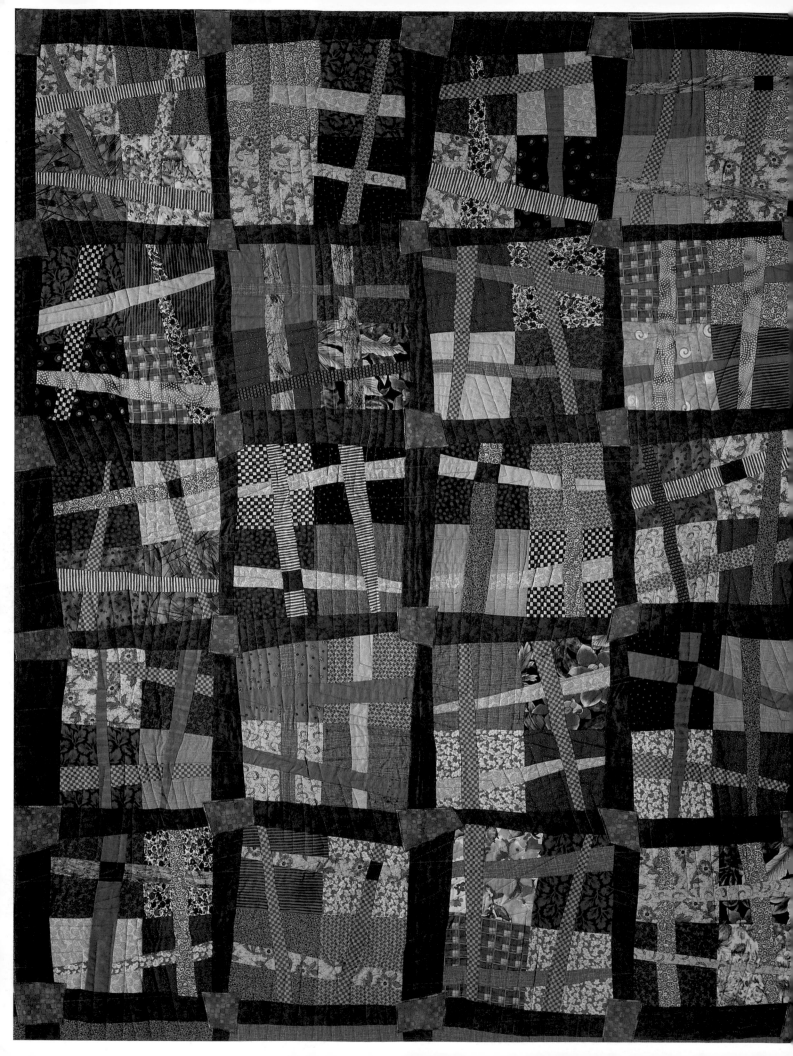

Preface

Several years ago, I began teaching a workshop to quiltmakers who wanted to stretch beyond normal quiltmaking boundaries. The class "come PLAY with me!" soon expanded from one day to two days, then more. It is the basis for this *Playtime* book. Students sometimes enrolled as a first step toward innovative piecing, intuitive color, and spontaneous design, hoping to discover playful joy through improvisational, impromptu "games," that is to say, "playing with blocks or designs or methods." Instead of playing at a table with a game board and movable pieces, these games are played at the sewing machine with thread and fabric and open minds.

With its playful approach, this concept of games is only a prelude. Where might the approach lead? That is limited only by your imagination. I believe the games are an entryway, and I look forward to seeing what may develop as the *Playtime* games are tested and taken to new heights. To me that's the purpose of *Playtime*–to release creative energies that have been there all the time, just awaiting the right moment to be set free. I take no responsibility for anything other than placing the ideas in motion; quiltmakers already own their abilities and talents.

From students, I continue to learn far more than they. Without a doubt, by the end of a session I am the one who has had the most fun. They do the stitching, but I get to watch as eyes gleefully twinkle the moment the light bulb goes on. It is a joy to see when a strict rule follower, who brought to class a firm code of ¼" seam allowances, impeccable grain lines, perfect color matches, and flawless points, comprehends that it is okay to be an outright rule breaker.

Enjoy the freedom. Play the games. May all your quilts be a creative delight; may your sandbox and playroom give you nothing but liberating design freedom.

Before the Game

Introduction

Play is something most of us have forgotten how to do. Day-to-day responsibilities limit time for amusement and entertainment. Watch a child play. As he imitates life, he learns how to grow into an adult. On the other hand, when an adult plays, he tries to remember how to be a child once more. I hope you are ready to adopt such a childlike mindset, for that is the perspective of *Playtime*.

As you discover how to play these games, you will also discover that many were designed for sharing, for playing with a friend. Yet others are equally enjoyed if played alone. Sometimes the fun comes in sharing results. Sometimes the fun is the sharing itself. No matter how you play, the games are loaded with unlimited possibilities that, as you adapt some of these methods to your own style, you will find and develop more and more creativity within yourself.

I suggest that you play each of the games in the order as given. As each game adds layer upon layer of information, methods "play" upon each other. By playing each game in turn, you may progress with greater proficiency. It will be to your advantage to read through each game's instructions before beginning any of the games. By reading the entire game, you will receive an overview of information. This is especially important for your first game.

Each game will have three distinct sections. First is Object of the Game, a section that gives the game's goal of play. Next you will find Game Plan, a section that lays out the strategy of the game. Finally, it's Your Move!—the instructions for creating the game.

My friend Sally K. Field read my first written instructions and then stitched quilts as book examples. Sometimes she made suggestions for another way to play a game or to accomplish a task, so I've included some of Sally's tips. You, the reader, and I, the author, both benefit from her ideas.

With playful antics at the sewing machine, scraplets of fabric and trailing strings all over the floor, and even a few tossed-aside candy wrappers, you can return to a child's big-eyed wonder at yet-to-be-learned possibilities.

Now that you are ready to play, there are a few things that are important to mention first. Of course, the purpose of *Playtime* is to free your creativity via liberating games at the sewing machine and on your design wall. But here are some basics you might need as you incorporate improvisational piecing into your quiltmaking.

The Playroom

The playroom is a place to capture your own playful mood. It may be the dining room table, or it may be a formal workspace. Wherever it is, analysis of your favorite way to work is important. I offer some questions that may help you define what kind of workspace is best for you.

• Do you like music? Soft background? Loud and noisy? What kind? Or does music distract you, and you work best in the quiet?

• What kind of lighting do you have? A well-lit area is kinder to the eyes. If you have fluorescent lighting, I suggest using a bulb that mimics natural lighting, called "full spectrum." Note any dark corners, and if you need additional lamps, shop around. Do you need additional lighting near your sewing machine? Great lamps are available that attach to desks or stand alone.

• Is your space arranged with as few steps as possible for designing, cutting, sewing, and ironing? Or is it helpful for you to get up and stretch by purposely locating your ironing surface or design area away from your sewing area?

• What about the height of your work surface? Is it ergonomically correct for you and your height?

• Is your equipment accessible and ready for work? Can you get to your stash of threads, fabrics, and accessories without moving stacks of other supplies or wasting time searching for a specific item?

After responding to these questions, you may need to revamp your space or relocate to best capture where you can create at your maximum level.

Keep an array of bobbins filled and ready to sew. Dianne keeps hers in a bon-bon box.

Use fabrics that excite.

Equipment and Supplies

To create quickly without hassle and frustration, a cleaned, well-oiled sewing machine in good working order is necessary. I am not a machinist, as any student will tell you. So, every January, when I schedule my yearly physical with my doctor, my sewing machine gets a check-up with the dealer at the same time. Without the care and feeding of this workhorse of a machine, my quiltmaking performance would suffer greatly.

Next, review your basic sewing tools. To prepare for piecing, fill three to four bobbins with a neutral piecing thread: gray, beige, taupe, or something that blends into your fabrics.

Additionally, it is efficient to have an array of colorful bobbins for switching to appliqué, or any other task in which the slightest bobbin thread might show through on the surface.

My favorite piecing thread is #60-weight embroidery thread, one that is not normally used for piecing but for fine embroidery. Why? It's very thin, so there is no bulk created by stitched seams. But more than that, the bobbin holds much more thread, so you have the luxury of sewing longer without refilling the bobbin.

For other supplies, you may need to have the following items on hand: freezer paper (the grocery store kind that comes in rolls), a lightweight fusible interfacing, and a lightweight paper-backed, iron-on fusible. It may also be handy to have either a water mister or a can of spray starch.

Game Fabrics

Use only fabrics that excite you. Let me repeat that. Use fabrics that make your heart jump a beat or two. Allow yourself to be visually stimulated by a delightful array of color. If you use just any old fabric to learn these playful methods, you will look at the finished piece as if it were just any old piece. Sometimes it is not easy to cut into beautiful fabrics for an exercise that you may or may not ever find useful. I contend that with ugly fabrics, you ordinarily end up with ugly combinations. Begin with excellence and you will have a far better shot at creating something that excels.

Overall, the ideal is to have a general assortment of fabrics. For certain games, a collection of hand-dyed, hand-painted, and batik-type fabrics work well. Bold prints may serve a game best, but so can geometrics, especially for finishing touches. It is not surprising that black-and-white prints, especially geometrics, create a nice end result. Of course, I suggest bright, intense, vibrant fabrics without grayed or dulled colors: real reds, glowing oranges, strong yellows, citrusy chartreuses, bright turquoises, ocean royals, etc. Include some large, bold prints and gutsy geometrics. Ethnic fabrics can add pizzazz!

For me, it's a personal preference to purchase yardage in ⅓-yard cuts. Anything larger creates a psychological hold on me, and I have a difficult time whacking into a great big beautiful yard of fabric. A gorgeous two-yard cut may lurk on a shelf for years, dying of old age. I've often thought that the best remedy for this strange stymieing reaction would be to take a pair of scissors, quickly sneak up on that large yardage, and cut it into bite-sized scraplets.

Ultimate fabric perfection would be a medley of fabrics with different motifs, designs, colors, and fiber content, all separated into whatever way best suits your style. If your fabric budget allows, more is always better, if only to look at a fabric's beauty.

For ease in piecing, I suggest 100 percent cottons, but if you are experienced with the methods and have done a lot of this type of

intuitive piecing, then try silks, rayons, lamés, and polyesters. All of these add texture, depth, and shine. Remember, in nearly all cases, silks and other shiny fabrics require fusing onto a soft, lightweight interfacing to keep the threads from raveling.

Now, let's talk scraps! Or better yet, let scraps talk to you. Let them speak by gathering scraps from recent exciting projects or other people, but please don't pick up oldies you no longer like or wouldn't *even* use in a current project. I find that having a basket of scraps to pour through or to dump on a table is most useful. When I prepare to create a new piece, I find that a scrap basket offers the most striking combinations, with surprising results, as tidbits of fabric land serendipitously next to each other.

This question is always asked: "What size should my scraps be?" That's easy. Are you able to sew another piece of fabric onto the scrap? If so, it is fair game (okay, I couldn't resist using the word). To my thinking, all scraps are useful. Long, slender, fat, large, medium, and even very small scraps offer a variety of scales and colors. Using scraps, especially those from other people, will encourage you to vary your palette.

When my scrap basket overflows into a totally jumbled mess, I find that one of the best things to do is sort the scraps. Sort the scraps? Yes, sort them. How? By color. By print. By scale. By whatever means of sorting or stacking works for you.

The benefits of organizing are threefold. First, organized scraps are more easily viewed. Second, the separating process often gives life to a new quilt. Third, as I go through the mass, submerged fabrics that are in conflict with each other surface. These can be segregated in the basket's confines or held in a separate box until I'm absolutely sure that it's time to give them away. It's a freeing thing to deliberately extract these no-longer-needed fabrics. By removing them, they won't clog up the basket's beauty. Plus, they may find a home in another quilt.

Many times I am asked, "How many fabrics do you use in a quilt?" Usually my response is, "Satisfy yourself." If your creativity requires a large selection, then use whatever you need to satisfy that desire. Because of the improvisational nature of the methods, the games will generally require more rather than less of your stash. Some game players have said, "Use every fabric you own!" Now my response is, "That's intimidating, so just use most of it!"

Wild Cards

"Wild Card" fabrics serve quilts in the same way that wild cards serve any game, acquiring any value you assign to them. Think of a Wild Card as a substitute fabric. Your objective is to identify fabrics in your mock-up that can be replaced. Often, one small fabric change will make the difference between an exciting piece and one that is acceptable, yet may not stir a strong emotional response.

You'll find serendipity in a scrap basket.

To employ Wild Cards, first you must recognize that something may be slightly wrong or out of place in your piece. Learn to see a possible inadequacy or deficiency.

Identify three things in your quilt: the where, what, and how. Where are the areas that might benefit from switching one or more fabrics? What scrap-basket tidbit do you have that you could use? These are easy-to-find Wild Cards. How you choose a Wild Card depends on color and scale, then design.

When you identify an area to be changed with a Wild Card, something unforeseen may occur. At the moment that you replace just one small piece of fabric, your quilt may begin to sparkle with excitement and beauty. Often, as lovely as I think my original fabric combination may be, a Wild Card switch makes it even better.

How do I locate these Wild Cards? For me, it's a matter of trial and error. Something will look wrong. It may be a learned process, seeing when something is not as it should be. It may be an innate perception, but whatever it is, I rely on that nagging feeling that "things just aren't right" to lead me through the design process. The nagging may take several days, or it may be something I see almost the minute a piece is put together. In all cases, I let the piece tell me.

After the piece has spoken and has said, "I'm not right, yet!" and, thereby needs some sort of replacement or revision, my favorite way is to go straight to my scrap basket. I lift out tidbits; I fold and pin these scraps over any offending fabric. When the "ah-ha" moment comes—the "*Yes*, that's the one!"—then the Wild Card is played.

How to Play
Warming Up with a Mock-up

What exactly is a mock-up? A mock-up is a layout, an actual arrangement of fabrics that are scaled to the same size you want to see in the completed piece. It is an overall plan, a visual, or a design for a finished quilt. In quiltmaking terms, it might be easier to define it by saying what a mock-up is not. It's not a layering of several yards or cuts of fabric that are disproportionate to what you want to see after you have done your stitching.

To make a mock-up, cut, fold, scrunch, or shape the fabrics so they are as close as possible to your desired finished sizes and shapes. If you ignore this most important step of creating a mock-up, it is likely that your finished quilt will be out of proportion.

My favorite way to begin a mock-up is with scraps. One at a time, I place scraps directly onto a background fabric. In this mock-up the background is a piece of flimsy, red, pleated-poly stuff.

If the quilt is small, however, I may lay the fabrics flat on a table instead of a background fabric. Both ways are excellent mock-up techniques. Both give a preview of the finished piece.

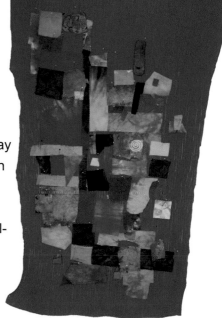

Doing a Mock-up

• Rule #1 of every game: Mock-up, mock-up, mock-up!

• Create a mock-up with pieces proportionate to what you want in the finished piece.

• Stand back and squint at your mock-up to "see" potential changes that should be made.

Playing the Angles

In general, make all your cuts with gentle angles rather than strong ones. A strong angle may be either acute (less than 45°) or obtuse (more than 90° and less than 180°).

Why do I insist on gentle angles? Look at what happens with a slight change of angle in the comparison of cut fabrics below. Strong angles create visual discomfort, while gentle angles create less tension.

Try for nonperpendicular lines and nonparallel lines when you cut. If your lines are either parallel or perpendicular, the randomness of your design will be limited. If your lines are parallel, especially when all the lines lean in one direction, the quilt will feel off balance and the viewer will find herself leaning.

Avoid strong angles.

Keep angles gentle.

Wallpaper Cuts

Have you ever wallpapered a room? If so, you know how to match two abutting panels. I employ the same technique in my quilts and call this a "wallpaper cut." This cut is used for the Hopscotch game, beginning on page 23.

When you prepare two fabrics for stitching by using this cutting method, the angles will match perfectly. To match the angles of two abutting panels of wallpaper, you overlap the panels and cut them together. I employ this same wallpaper cutting technique when I prepare two pieces for stitching together. To make the cut, simply overlap two pieces, with both of them *right side up*. For the bottom piece, check to see that there is enough fabric for the cut. Then cut through both pieces at once with your rotary cutter.

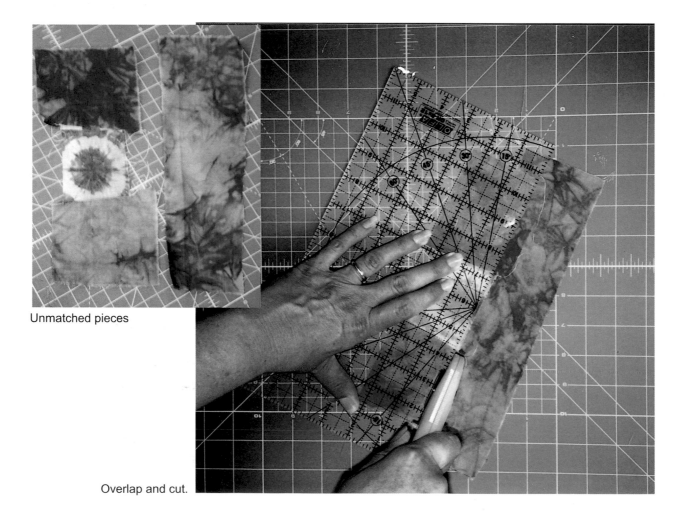

Unmatched pieces

Overlap and cut.

Making Allowances

Contrary to using the normal ¼" seam allowance suggested or required by most quilt-making methods, a ⅛" seam allowance will work very nicely for many of the games. You ask why? It's a visual thing. If a fabric piece works in a mock-up, it follows that the finished piece would be much smaller if a ¼" seam allowance were used.

Although you are piecing intuitively as you play, your own techniques and skills from all your previous quiltmaking need to be incorporated. Often, it is thought that improvisation means "anything goes." Not so. Instead, it means that you may develop your piece in whatever direction the improvisation leads you; but you still need clean finishes, pressed seams, and nice straight stitching.

Game Plan for Ironing

The sentence "The iron is my friend" is one I often speak aloud to myself when creating a new quilt top. Thankfully, the iron has coerced many fabrics into place, especially when used in conjunction with what I call my "secret weapon,"

a can of spray starch or a water mister. These two items have gotten me out of many fabric jams and helped to make my quilts of innumerable fabrics lie totally flat.

What kind of iron suits you best? Personally I never use steam, because with steam I frequently burn myself. My preference is an inexpensive manual shut-off iron, so that, when I knock it off the ironing board, it doesn't cost an arm and a leg to replace. Also, I enjoy switching back and forth from pressing pieced areas to using the iron for machine appliqué.

When you press, always consider what you want to see the most. The iron helps reinforce your visual preference. Thus, you may violate many of the pressing rules you learned early in your quiltmaking journey. To make a fabric piece come toward you (pop rather than recede), you may press the seam allowance toward a lighter colored fabric, whereas with normal quilt rules, you press toward the darker fabric. The time to make the decision on how to press is at the point of creation. It is not critical to decide in advance.

Playtime Tips

• Don't think too much.
• Fast counts.
• Allow your hands to be your guides.
• Give your color-selecting brain a rest.
• For more fun, find a friend (or two or three) to share the experience.
• Fabric trading is encouraged. To increase your stash, you may beg, borrow, or trade.
• On the way to your sewing machine, munch a chocolate bar and grab a handful of gummy bears for exciting energy.

• The author is not responsible for your fabric bill!

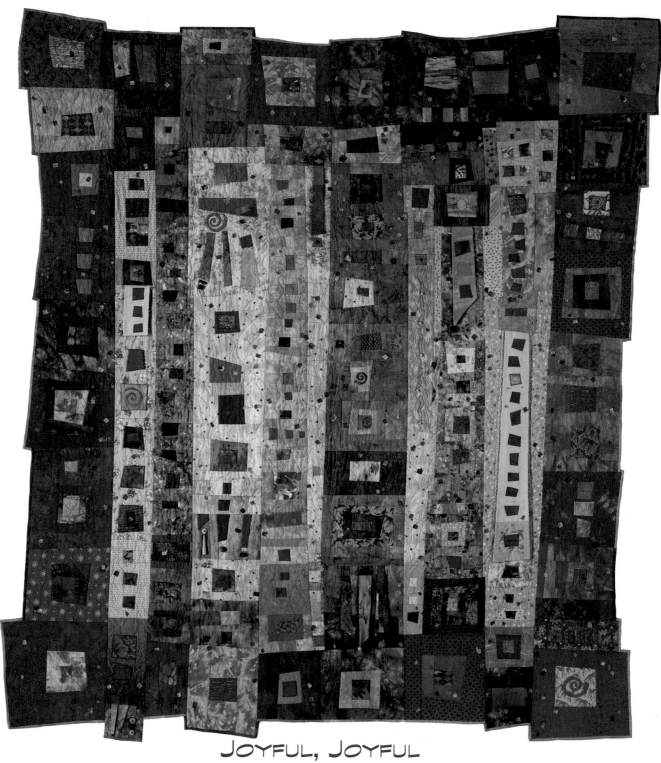

JOYFUL, JOYFUL
74½" x 86½"
Made by the author.
All of these vertical runs began as teaching samples. The happy colors
caused Dianne to hum Beethoven's engaging melody of joy.

Let the Games Begin

Hopscotch

Object of the Game

Hopscotch is a great game to get you started playing with fabric in preparation for improvisational quiltmaking. The first time you play the game, it's not necessary to spend time futzing with it. Just begin. Later, when you know where the game may lead, come back and create another game, in a different colorway, if need be.

For the Hopscotch game we learned as children, the object was to complete a course chalked on a sidewalk by alternately hopping on one foot, then two feet, and skipping over certain areas. Similarly, when you play Hopscotch, you create a "run" of fabrics, skipping over each "unblock," much like playing on a chalked sidewalk. If you look closely, the Hopscotch block resembles a Courthouse variation of the Log Cabin block. Note the difference between a traditional block and one that is altered for Hopscotch play.

Traditional Courthouse Log Cabin block

Hopscotch block

The game's object is to complete a fast and easy "run" of fabrics. A normal run is vertical and it consists of at least five to seven unblocks encased in irregularly shaped logs. Hopscotch runs may also be used as a border for another game.

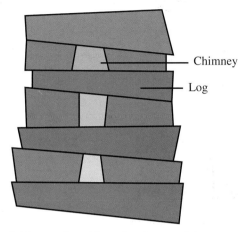

Unblocks (chimneys) and logs (background) in a run of Hopscotch.

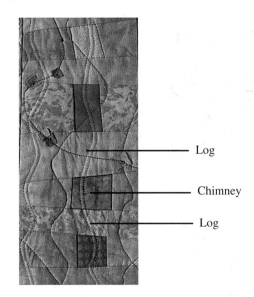

The detail from JOYFUL, JOYFUL shows the unblocks (chimneys) and logs (background) in a run of Hopscotch. Note that there is only one log above and one log below each unblock and that the run is created vertically from bottom to top.

Game Plan

If you recall from the Introduction, the game plan provides the strategies for how to play a game. Strategies include selecting a colorway and creating a mock-up to determine the sizes and shapes of your pieces.

Colorways

For quick play, here are two simple colorway options for the unblocks. An easy color choice is to cut the unblocks from one color and the logs from another. For variety, use gradations of the same color for either the unblocks or the logs.

In OXYMORON: RANDOM ORDER, the unblocks are all black, and the logs are cut from one color family—red, reddish pink, and hot pink.

Detail from OXYMORON: RANDOM ORDER. Black unblocks are set in logs of one color family. The full quilt is pictured on page 28.

The mint green run in a detail from JOYFUL, JOYFUL is an example of unblocks that are different colors with background fabrics from the same color family. Use color families for Hopscotch runs. The full quilt is pictured on page 22.

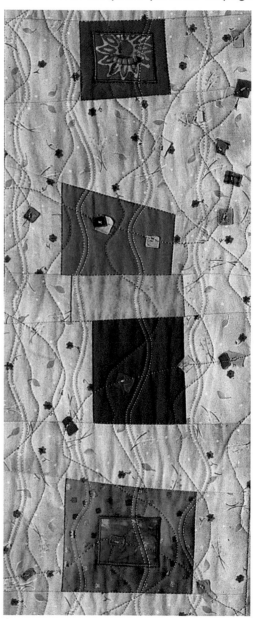

Detail from JOYFUL, JOYFUL. The unblocks are different colors with mint green background fabrics (the same color family). The full quilt is pictured on page 22.

Mock-up

Be sure to create a mock-up before you sew. To create good proportion, *always* cut, fold, or scrunch the unblocks to your envisioned size and shape and place them on a background fabric that is also cut to your desired finished size. This may be one of the most important techniques to learn when playing the *Playtime* games.

Mock-up Examples

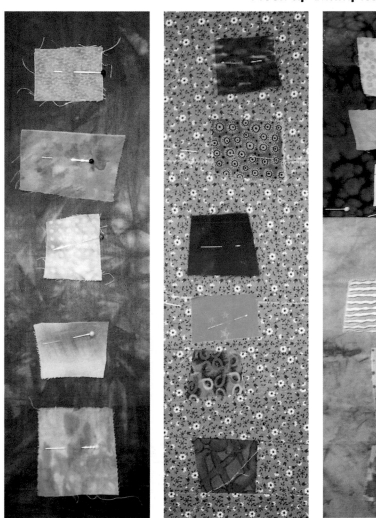

Mock-up examples with hand-dyed fabrics and calicos

A good mock-up of a Hopscotch game followed by a better example. See how the mock-up becomes much stronger with just a few fabric Wild Card changes.

Your Move!

1. Start with one scissor-cut unblock that has gentle angles and no perpendicular or parallel lines.

2. In your mind's eye, extend the top and bottom lines to the right and left of the unblock.

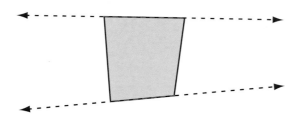

3. Cut the right and left background logs by using the extended lines as your guides. To be safe, when you cut, add a bit of fabric for wiggle room. Then sew the logs to the unblock and press the seam allowances toward the unblock so the unblock pops rather than recedes.

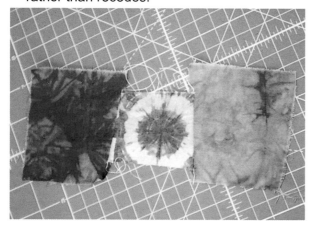

4. Rough-cut a log for the bottom of the unblock unit, using wallpaper cuts as described on page 20. Match the edges of the log and the unblock unit and sew the two components together. Press seam allowances toward the log, making sure that you have pressed your stitching line carefully.

5. Repeat this process to cut, match, and sew a top log in place.

6. Create a second three-part unblock unit consisting of an unblock and a right and left log. Use a wallpaper cut to match this sewn unit above the first Hopscotch block, then sew the two pieces together. Add another connecting log to the top as before.

7. One at a time, continue adding logs and unblock units, until you have a run of at least five unblocks. Note that, for improvisational methods, production piecing does not work well because you cannot change the angles or designs.

Save this run for a later use. It can be incorporated into another quilt by adding other components to it. Be sure to leave the edges untrimmed and messy, just like this example.

Keeping It Spontaneous

• Sometimes the best example is one showing what not to do. The first mock-up in the figure below is too perfect. The unblocks are almost square. If this quilt were sewn, there would be no spontaneity, and the run would have no exciting movement.

• Instead of using just one fabric for your background, why not use several that are similar?

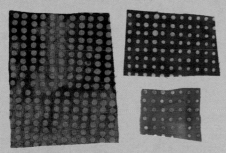

I've named these fabrics "transitionals."

Transitional Fabrics

• By combining similar fabrics, you can use up older pieces, and your quilt will have more movement and life.

• If you run out of background fabric in the middle of creating your piece, transitioning to another fabric works wonders. Such accidents provide much more free-form excitement.

Winning at Hopscotch

• Vary the width of each log to make almost a fan-shaped wedge. If the log is smaller at the edge of the right side, make it larger at the left side. Then, to vary your piece, reverse it by making it larger at the right side and smaller at the left, yet with no wedge like another.

• It is important that you visually extend the top and bottom lines of the unblock. If you find that the lines extend to a tiny point at one end and a very wide-open expanse at the other, the angle of the unblock is too sharp.

Compare these angles:

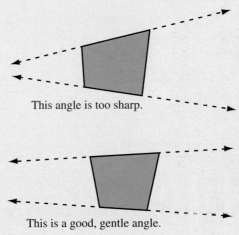

This angle is too sharp.

This is a good, gentle angle.

• Production piecing does not work well for Hopscotch.

• Trim only after the entire upward run is finished and you are ready to sew another piece to the run. Our quilt-making tendency is to clean up the edges, but this is not a good idea for improv piecing.

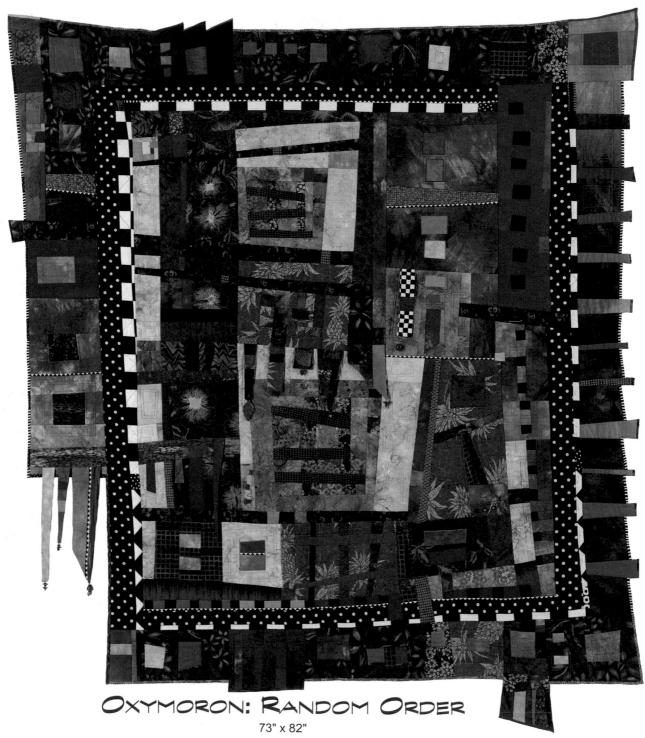

Oxymoron: Random Order

73" x 82"

Made by the author.

Dianne's quilting games began with this quilt.

KITES
26½" x 26½"
Made by Peggy Ireland Elliot, Cumberland, Maine.
Peggy created a tiny game of Hopscotch as an
interior border for a Pinwheel pattern.

BAMBOO SEA

26" x 27"

Made by Peggy Ireland Elliot, Cumberland, Maine.
Peggy combined several large Hopscotch blocks
into this triangular shape. She hand dyes many of
her own fabrics.

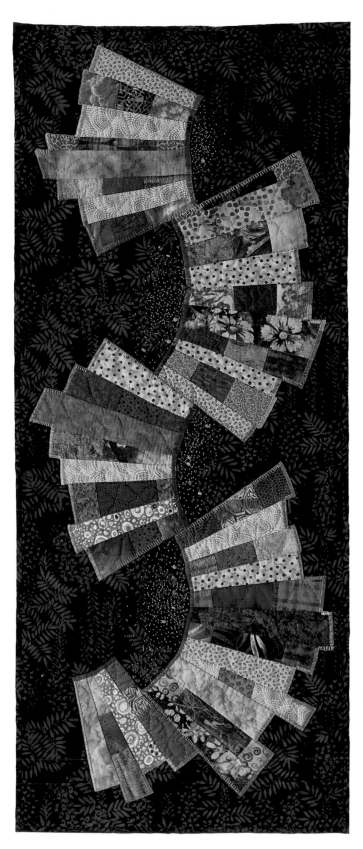

FLOWER FRACTALS

18¼" x 44"

Made by Alice Hobbs Parsons, Belmont, Maine,
and owned by Barbara and Galen Plummer.
Alice opted to give the game a Japanese flavor by
fanning the units with opposing curves.
She then added a beautiful hand-embroidered
blanket stitch with delicate beading.

EMILY
52" x 53"
Made by Audrey M. Kierman, Queensbury, New York, and owned by Emily Warner.
On a July day in 1998, Audrey bravely enrolled in the first "game" workshop. This is the first quilt from any game
instructions, giving the author hope that there was something to these methods after all.

Let's Play
69" x 84½"
Made by Hilary Cannon Anderson, Bloomington, Indiana.
Hilary added more games as she collaborated with her nine-year-old daughter, Erika,
who delightfully holds her own with designs at the sewing machine.

TIC-TAC-TOE

86½" x 87½"

Made by the author.

Dianne's choice of background colors creates multiple borders.

The inserts of the exterior blocks invade the final borders.

Tic-Tac-Toe

Object of the Game

The goal of Tic-Tac-Toe is to create the illusion of a Four-Patch block with vertical and horizontal inserts. The inserts are similar to a pencil-sketched Tic-Tac-Toe game.

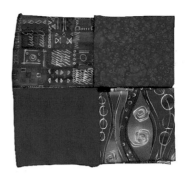

Four hot colors: combine a deep, hot pink with a fire engine red of the same intensity and two red-orange prints in a different scale.

Game Plan

Tic-Tac-Toe begins with four perfectly matched squares. The playful inserts that create the Tic-Tac-Toe block will quickly skew the block. Ultimately, the perfectly matched center intersection lets the eye trick itself into seeing a perfect Four-Patch block. For example, look at my quilt entitled TIC-TAC-TOE on the previous page. Upon an initial quick viewing of the quilt, it appears that all the inserted strips and the Four-Patch blocks match. Upon closer inspection, you actually see that nearly nothing matches, because your eye saw incorrectly at first glance. This is a matter of illusion, of fooling the eye.

Four cool colors: combine two dark and two medium hunter greens. Use a change of scale in the prints to give diversity and depth.

Colorways

At right, I offer three colorway options for the four different squares in your Four-Patch blocks. Always vary your scales and prints for more interesting combinations.

Select two different fabrics of one tone and two of another for your Four-Patch background. If you opt to use any true stripes for your fabrics, I suggest that you cut your squares on a slight bias, because the straight-grain lines of a stripe can sometimes interfere with the insert strips.

Four "no-colors": a checkerboard effect is created with black-and-white background fabrics, offering many colorway options for the insert strips.

Colorways for Tic-Tac-Toe inserts

Before you proceed with cutting and sewing the Four-Patch squares, select fabrics for the four inserts. As a general guide, use opposite temperatures. If you choose hot colors for the background squares, select cool colors for the inserts, or vice versa. Fabric variety works well for the game of Tic-Tac-Toe. I suggest that you select four different fabrics in similar colors for each pair of inserted strips. The inserted strips represent the parallel lines in Tic-Tac-Toe. Because these pairs of inserts are not truly parallel, let's call them "unparallels."

Remember, for Tic-Tac-Toe, the various shades of lilac and purple may work as either cool or hot colors, depending on how you com-bine them. If combined with blues or greens, they may take on attributes of hot colors, whereas if combined with reds, they may appear cool. Color matching is unimportant for Tic-Tac-Toe's unparallel inserts. If at first you find it difficult to combine a true red with a deep orange, please trust me that it will work in your finished block. Keep in mind that it is the inten-sity of the shade that makes the pairing work.

Try to locate four different scales, patterns, and designs of fabric, but keep them simple enough that they do not interfere with the Four-Patch designs. These inserts are the reason the game is called Tic-Tac-Toe, and they should pop out from the background rather than drop into it.

Colorways

• A good way to choose the inserted unparallels is to find pairs that increase or decrease the hue's intensity. That means finding a similar color family for the two strips in each pair.

• Your first thought may be that cool colors consist only of different shades of greens and blues. The range is actually large and includes turquoises, aquas, periwinkles, and some purples.

• Select four hot colors for inserts if you chose four cool colors for your background.

• Black-and-whites work as inserts for almost any color of block. If you selected a Four-Patch of black-and-whites, colored inserts seem to work best for your paired inserts.

• Select four cool colors for your Four-Patch background of hot colors.

• Create a checkerboard effect by alternating dark, predominantly black fabrics with light, predominantly white fabrics.

If you choose "no-colors" (neutrals) for your Four-Patch, select any color that you like for the inserts, but keep the selection narrowed to two color pairs that are similarly colored.

If you select a strong orange print for one of the unparallel inserts in the pair, pick a strong color, such as a strong red-orange print, for its companion. A pale color is not strong enough to carry the weight of the deep orange. However, the second pair on top can be two lighter fabrics in pinky-red, and again, they need to be different scales and designs.

Mock-up

Before you cut your fabrics or stitch them together, create a mock-up by scrunching or folding your fabrics into whatever block size you want for your completed Four-Patch. By scrunching, you can see how the color and scale relationships in the block will look.

Combine two different red colors with two different orange colors.

Your Move!

Cutting and sewing Four-Patches

1. Cut four squares any size between 4" and 7". I suggest that you do not make the squares much smaller than 3" or larger than 7".
2. Piece your four squares together in the normal fashion, using a ¼" seam allowance. Take care to match the seams at the center intersection *precisely*. Press seam allowances according to your preference.

Stitching Tic-Tac-Toe inserts

Before proceeding, please read all of this section on stitching your Tic-Tac-Toe inserts. It is *imperative* that you use ⅛" seam allowances when you sew this game. It will take four seams to stitch the insertions into the segments of the Four-Patch. If you were to use a normal ¼" seam allowance, you would remove a full inch

This mock-up shows cool unparallels on a hot Four-Patch background.

of the Four-Patch background. Instead, if you sew with a ⅛" seam allowance, you remove only ½" of the background. The block skews very quickly with a ⅛" seam allowance, so think how much it would skew if you used a normal ¼" seam.

To sew the inserts to the Four-Patch background, sew the left vertical insert to the extreme left background piece (if you are right-handed, begin on the left and work to the right). Sew the right vertical insert to the extreme right background piece (if you are left-handed, begin on the right and work toward the left).

1. Do a mock-up of the four insert fabrics with your sewn Four-Patch block. Decide which of the pairs you want to recede and which pair you want to dominate.

This mock-up shows that red-violet inserts will recede and blue-violet inserts will dominate.

2. Whichever pair you select to recede will be sewn into the Four-Patch first. Cut the four insert fabrics into strips approximately 2" wide by the finished length of your Four-Patch plus 4". The added length means you will have long tails after the strips have been sewn in place.

3. On your Four-Patch background, make two vertical cuts, gently angled into an uneven V. These will be called "V-cuts." Be careful, as you make your V-cut, not to cross the vertical center line or get too near the block's exterior edges.

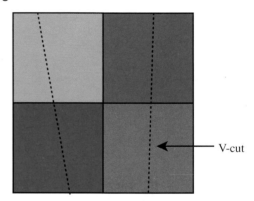

V-cut

4. You will now have three pieces of Four-Patch background. Keep them in order as you cut.

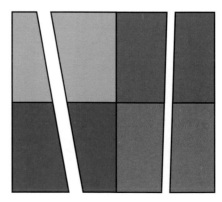

5. Align the inserts with the Four-Patch background pieces, creating wedge shapes that are wider at the top and narrower at the

bottom. Leave extra fabric tails 2" above as well as 2" below the background.

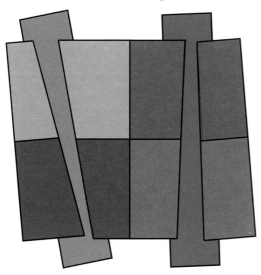

6. With fabrics right side up and with the pieces laid out the way you want them, visually mark a stitching line for the first insert by placing a ruler where you want the first seam to be.

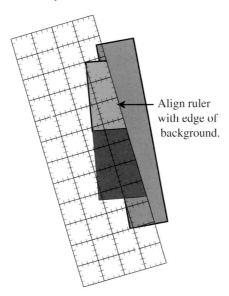

Align ruler with edge of background.

7. Remove the background piece and gently move the ruler ⅛" for a seam allowance (⅛" to the left if you are right-handed. If you are left-handed

and you began on the right, move the ruler ⅛" to the right). Now, with a rotary cutter, cut *only the insert* along this new line. You will not be cutting anything away from the background.

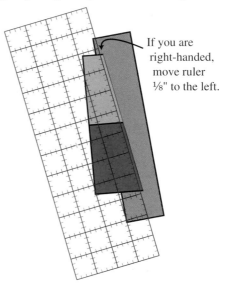

If you are right-handed, move ruler ⅛" to the left.

8. With the fabrics right side up, lay the middle section of the background onto the first insert. Place the strip so that the insert is either wider at the top or at the bottom. At the same time, eyeball the horizontal seam lines of the Four-Patch background so they are not totally mis-matched.

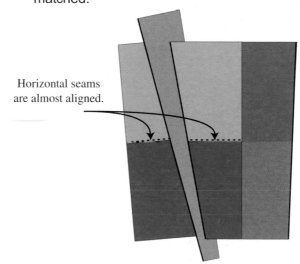

Horizontal seams are almost aligned.

9. Stitch the second side of the insert to the center section of your Four-Patch block. (Press seam allowances toward the insert, causing it to come forward, creating the Tic-Tac-Toe grid. If you press away from the inserts, they appear to recede behind the Four-Patch block).

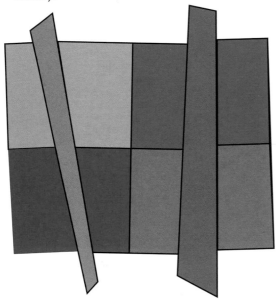

10. Rotate your newly created Four-Patch block a quarter turn, and make two new V-cuts.

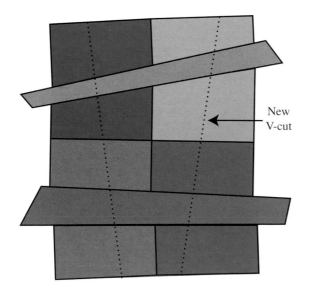

New V-cut

11. Repeat steps 5 through 7 for cutting and sewing the second insert in the pair. Again, press seam allowances toward the insert. Your newly created Four-Patch block will be similar to the one in the photo, but not exactly like it. Do not cut off the tails.

12. Create at least three more blocks for a small wallhanging. Make each new block compatible with the previous one, if you liked it when you finished. If not, rethink your colorways for background squares or for inserts. When you have four blocks completed, put them on your design wall and play with their placement, moving each block around until you are pleased with the design.

13. Now, you are faced with several decisions. Should you make these blocks square and use sashing? Or, should you square them up and not sash? Or, should you just sew blocks together?

What if you want all the blocks to remain uneven unblocks, yet you want to connect them with sashing? Can you do that? The answer is yes. The sashing will also be sewn in unevenly.

To appliqué the tails to the borders, as was done in TIC-TAC-TOE, gently rip out a portion of the stitched tails at the edge of the block. Stitch the sashing to the Four-Patch block, then appliqué the tails to the sashing.

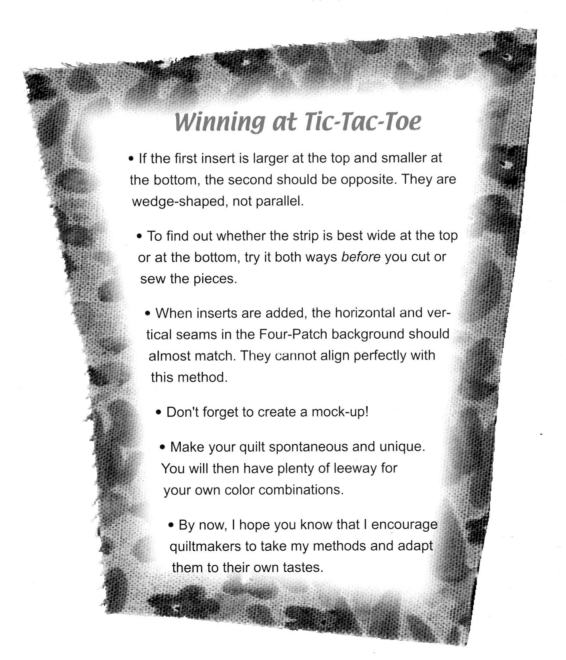

Winning at Tic-Tac-Toe

• If the first insert is larger at the top and smaller at the bottom, the second should be opposite. They are wedge-shaped, not parallel.

• To find out whether the strip is best wide at the top or at the bottom, try it both ways *before* you cut or sew the pieces.

• When inserts are added, the horizontal and vertical seams in the Four-Patch background should almost match. They cannot align perfectly with this method.

• Don't forget to create a mock-up!

• Make your quilt spontaneous and unique. You will then have plenty of leeway for your own color combinations.

• By now, I hope you know that I encourage quiltmakers to take my methods and adapt them to their own tastes.

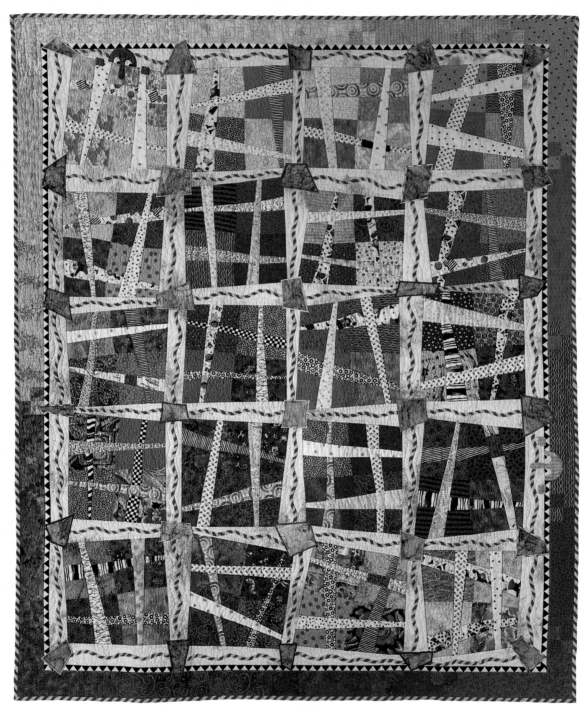

INSIDE THE RAINBOW

60¾" x 73½"

Made by Barbara Baume, Southington, Connecticut.
Barbara's quilt is definitely a rainbow of color in an array of
yellows, reds, and Caribbean turquoises.

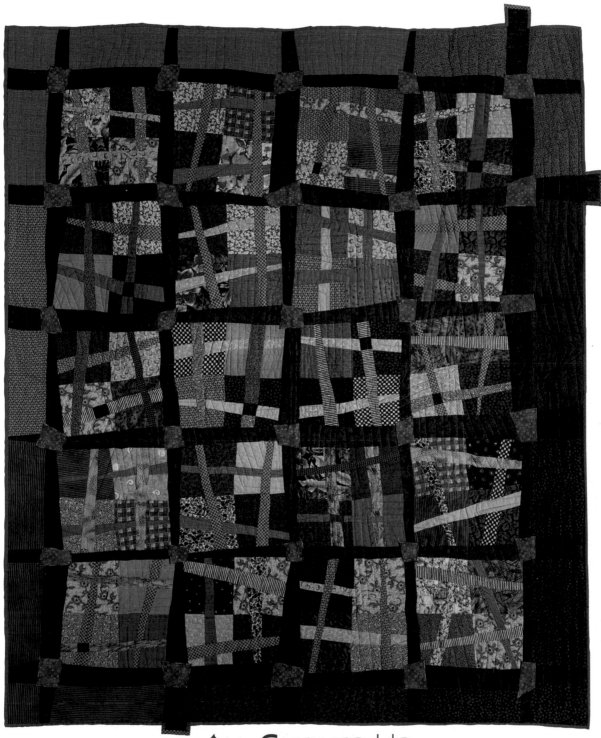

ALL SKEWED UP
65" x 78"

Made by Linda Lawrence Neustadt, South Grafton, Massachusetts.
Linda's hot-pink posts glow on top of the many blue Four-Patch blocks.
The blues were given life when Linda included a few pink squares in the background.

SCRAP HAPPY
32½" x 32¼"
Made by Priscilla Read, San Leandro, California.
Priscilla designed her quilt in a large variety of
colors and scales and created a delightfully
energetic quilt. Photo by Priscilla Read.

INDECISION

30⅛" x 30⅛"

Made by Sally K. Field, Hampden, Maine.

Sally actually played several real games of Tic-Tac-Toe to determine quilting lines.

The quilt still couldn't decide whether it wanted to play Hopscotch or Tic-Tac-Toe.

PLANET GAMES

43½" x 42¼"

Made by Peggy Ireland Elliott, Cumberland, Maine.

Peggy created a new configuration of Tic-Tac-Toe with appliquéd circles
behind the V-cut inserts and as posts for her uneven sashing.

Detail from
Tic-Tac-Toe,
page 34.

Detail from
Inside the Rainbow
page 42.

Detail from
All Skewed Up
page 43.

Dangler 1
15" x 21"
Made by the author.
Dianne plays Pin the Tail on the Donkey.

Pin the Tail on the Donkey

Object of the Game

For several years now, I have added details, such as beading, sequins, torn-apart jewelry, and scraps of fabrics to quilts. One of the thrills of intuitive piecing is that accidents nearly always occur, and it was quite by accident that I discovered the game of Pin the Tail on the Donkey.

The object of the game is to create active motion in your quilt with either inserted or freely dangling tails. DANGLER 1 is the first quilt I made using these whimsical additions that provide action, movement, and possibly a bit of friction to a quilt–all of which add interest and excitement. Tails are delightful attachments that do not conform to most quiltmaking techniques. Capricious in nature, they are fun to create.

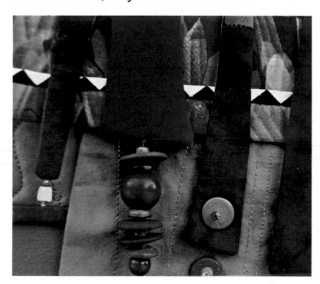

Detail from DANGLER 1

Game Plan

This active motion may be achieved in a couple of ways. The first way is to create actual three-dimensional pieces that may be single, double, or multiple tails. Tails in 3-D expand quiltmaking techniques and add architectural structure to a flat fabric surface. The other way to create this visual motion is by use of inserted tails. By sewing in the tail-shape, motion is implied. It tricks the viewer's eye into seeing a tail, albeit a stationary one.

Colorways

As an overall game plan for playing Pin the Tail on the Donkey, make a few decisions before sewing. Don't take a great deal of time deliberating over choices. It is okay to create and sew a few mistakes, and when you do, save those mistakes for another day's use.

For colorways, imagine a tail's personality. Should it be feisty and important, or should it be shy and reserved? This analysis of information tells you whether or not a tail should be emphasized as an important detail in your quilt.

If you want to call attention to the tail, find a bold fabric, or piece together several fabrics into one attention-getting unit. Perhaps you might try out important fabrics that are not used elsewhere in the quilt, such as crisp black-and-whites, bold geometrics, or an unlikely color or scale. Consider embellishments of embroidery or beads to add emphasis. For a quiet tail, one with less importance, use a fabric that blends with the fabrics around it.

TAILS OF PLAYTIME

15" x 20"

Made by the author.

Dianne sketched a possible design and then created the quilt. She tried every kind of tail, pieced and inserted, with layer upon layer of multi-tails.

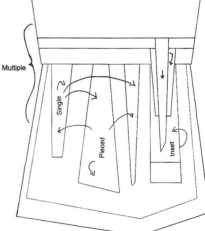

Mock-up

In every case, remember to do a mock-up. Tails need to be arranged and viewed in proportion to your finished piece before you sew. When you add tails, please audition them for color, scale, and proportion. Such try-outs are a key to creating a successful use of these fun fabrics. The sketches below offer some ideas for your mock-up. You can start with these, then see where your imagination takes you.

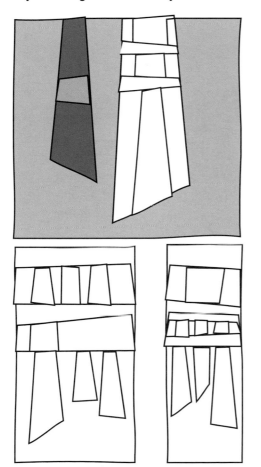

Use sketches to get your imagination going.

The mock-up can have tails that are emphasized and others that blend in with the background fabrics. Sometimes your Pin the Tail

block works beautifully with a Hopscotch block, as in the following design-wall pieces.

This is a thinking stage, with Hopscotch and Pin the Tail on the Donkey placed on a design wall. Photo by Ted Blank, Portsmouth, New Hampshire.

Creating Motion

• Create motion with color by layering a series of simple tails, each in a different color. When organized into a group, such a composite offers wonderful excitement to your quilt.

• A quiet, inserted tail that recedes into the background adds soft, gentle movement to your quilt, motion that is not there, but implied.

Your Move!
Inserted tails

1. To cut inserted tails and their backgrounds, use the wallpaper-cutting techniques described on page 20.
2. Follow your mock-up as you stitch the inserted tails into their backgrounds.

Dangling tails

1. Making a dangling tail is like sewing together a miniature pillowcase. With right sides together, stitch three sides, leaving the top open.
2. Trim the two corner seam allowances to about 1/8", then carefully turn the tail right side out.
3. Pin the tails to your quilt top, adjusting them so they dangle according to the rules of gravity, and sew them in place.

Tail Shapes

• Tails may be created in many shapes.

• Tail ends can slant in either direction, or they can be long and pointy.

• Make some tails large at the top and small at the bottom, then offset that effect by inverting some shapes so they are small at the top and large at the bottom.

• Tails that don't obey the laws of gravity create a windswept effect and hang unnaturally. If, upon completion of your entire quilt top, you find that the tails do not hang correctly, now is the time to use a seam ripper. Hang your quilt top on a wall and adjust the tails before you sandwich and quilt your piece.

Turning Tails

• My favorite turning tool is an enamel chopstick. It has a thin, blunt end that, if you are careful when you use it, will not punch through the sewn end during turning. The skinnier the tail, however, the harder it may be to turn. A useful tip came from a student in Berkeley, California. She sews together her little "pillowcase." Then she inserts an oversized plastic straw into it. Next, beginning at the outside of the sewn end, she gently pushes her chopstick into and through the straw, easily turning the fabric.

Pin the Tail on the Donkey Quilts

DANGLING PARTICIPLES
35" x 39"
Made by the author.
Dianne says this quilt is an example
of actively misusing the grammatical
definition of a dangling participle.

SOLUTIONS (GRAY)?
51" x 50"
Made by the author.
This quilt has several tails that are made not only of
fabric but of beads, plastics, and combinations of
other assorted things, such as silk yo-yos.

HIDDEN AGENDA

30" x 26½"
Made by the author.
Dianne created a feeling of fanciful play and visual
action as air moves about her three-dimensional quilt.

Detail from HIDDEN AGENDA. Peek under the
top quilt to see five other little quilts secretly
hanging from a fat fabric-covered hanging
rod. In all, there are seven quilts in one.

Hot Seat Musical Chairs

47½" x 42½"

Made by the author.

Dianne plays Musical Chairs by skewing the blocks on point.

Musical Chairs

Object of the Game

In the game of Musical Chairs, you will "walk" fabric pieces in an orderly fashion around an arrangement of nine blocks. The game could also be called "orderly disorder," because its objective is to alternate doing something orderly and then doing something very disorderly.

The game's other objective is to create a quilt by selecting a compatible grouping of fabrics without really knowing how the quilt will look when completed. The process is fun and fast, and gives great satisfaction to play.

Game Plan

The quilt is made up of nine quick blocks. Your first strategy will be to select fabrics for the blocks.

Colorways

Real Musical Chairs eliminates players one at a time. In Musical Chairs colorways, you begin with more "players" than you will end up with. Begin by gathering an assortment of 18 to 20 fabrics that look to you like they go together. Select by colorway, by print design, by scale, or by a combination of these. For more information, see Colorway Options on page 61.

After choosing an assortment of 18 to 20 fabrics, eliminate a couple of them, distilling the assortment down to 16 fabrics. Don't agonize over this. Just do it.

Now it is time to get out a Wild Card, a "zinger" fabric to replace one of your 16 fabrics. A zinger is a fabric that doesn't seem to belong. It's something slightly out of place. Let the new rule-breaking quiltmaker in you take over from the rule-keeping quiltmaker and see what happens.

Determine what size to cut your squares; 8" or 9" is a good size. I recommend that you don't go much under 7" or over 11" for these squares. Cut one square from each selected fabric. Then, once more, narrow your selection. Select only 10 of your 16 cut squares. Take a hard look at how they might look together, but keep your Wild Card zinger fabric in the mix. Remember to keep a variety of colors, scales, and print designs.

Stack the 10 selected squares in an order that varies the color, scale, and design. The bottom fabric will be your Wild Card. After you've laid out the first nine fabrics, you will have the option of exchanging Wild Cards for pieces anywhere in the layout. As you stack, watch out that you do not use one strong light or one strong dark fabric next to another. Do not stack two similar fabrics next to each other, because the fabrics blend into one another, and something like color-bleeding occurs. When you are satisfied with your selection of 10 fabrics, make another stack of your discards to the right of your selected fabric stack. When you stack both groups, leave a ½" viewing space in order to see the combinations.

For this game, do not create a mock-up before you play. Instead, just begin the game. Enjoy!

Your Move!

1. Your first move is to gather working supplies that are needed to play Musical Chairs. Have the following items ready:
   - 1 to 1½ yards of white or light-colored flannel, something that can be drawn on with indelible ink
   - black, medium-point, indelible-ink pen
   - graph paper 12" x 12"–any size grid is fine
   - a hard surface approximately 14" x 14", for transporting small fabric pieces. (A piece of cardboard or a small rotary cutting board works nicely.)

2. On the flannel, draw your Musical Chairs game board. With your black indelible-ink pen, draw nine squares in a 3 x 3 configuration, making each square approximately the same size as one of your cut squares.

Do not waste time drawing exact dimensions with a ruler. Leave space between each sketched square so you can manipulate your design while keeping each square separated. Number the squares from 1 to 9 for easy identification.

Drawing your Musical Chairs game pieces

1. Draw, then cut a graph-paper square *exactly* the same size as one of your cut fabric squares. This will be your template.
2. On the template, draw two almost vertical and two almost horizontal lines. None should be parallel or leaning in the same direction.
3. Number each of the nine small segments (these will be your game pieces) and draw an arrow pointing up in one corner of the template.

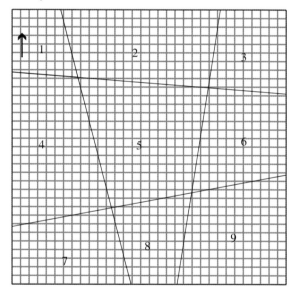

Cutting out your game pieces

1. Only 9 of the 10 fabrics will actually be used for the first trial layout of your blocks, but you will cut game pieces from all 10 fabrics.
2. Stack your squares according to the order in which you arranged them earlier, placing the Wild Card on the bottom.
3. Because it's not easy to rotary cut a full stack of 10 fabrics accurately, create two or three stacks of your selected fabrics. In preparation for rotary cutting, be careful to stack one fabric *perfectly* on top of another.

4. Fold the graph paper template along the right-side vertical line. Place the folded paper onto one stack of fabric. Align your ruler next to the fold and slice through the stack with a rotary cutter. Take care not to slice through the paper. Repeat this process until you have sliced through all the fabrics in each stack along this fold. Remember, take care not to slice through the paper, or you will have to tape it back together.

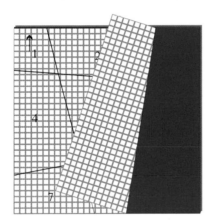

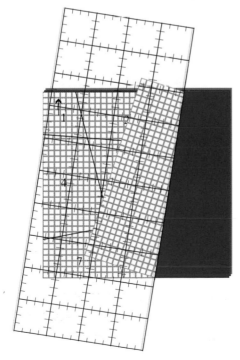

5. Unfold the paper template and refold it along the left-side vertical line. Use this folded line as a guide to rotary cut through all the stacked fabrics.

6. Unfold the paper template again and rotate the stacked fabric with the template a quarter turn. Repeat the folding and cutting process for the two almost horizontal lines on each stack. Your fabric squares should now be cut into nine game pieces.

7. Place your unfolded paper template onto your 14" x 14" transporting surface (the cardboard or a small rotary cutting board). Cover the template with the cut segments, *keeping the fabrics stacked in their original order.*

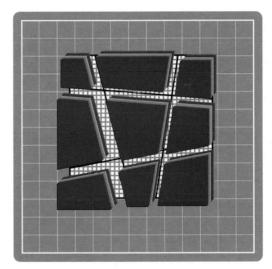

8. Place your flannel game board flat on a table or the floor, ready to play your game pieces.

Rules of the game

Keep in mind that the tenth Wild Card fabric in your stack will be left over because you plan to have only nine blocks when you finish arranging the pieces. Observe the following general rules for the first round of play:

- Place each game piece on the flannel game board in the square corresponding to its position on the template.
- Place all of the #1 pieces on your game board before placing the #2 game pieces. Then place all of the #3 pieces and so on, until you have placed all nine game pieces.
- ***Musical Chairs Secret Code:*** The game piece number corresponds to the number of the square that starts the game play for each stack.

Round one . . . orderly play

In the first round of Musical Chairs, you will play by the rules in an orderly manner. Here goes!

1. Place game piece #1 from your first fabric in position #1 in the first game-board block. Place piece #1 of your second fabric in the second block on your game board. Continue placing pieces sequentially until nine of the #1 game pieces from the fabrics are positioned on the game board.

2. Begin in the *second block* on your game board to place piece #2 of your first fabric.

Continue placing the pieces sequentially. When you get to the #9 block, you will have the #2 piece left over from your ninth fabric. Go back to the first block on the game board and put it in position #1.

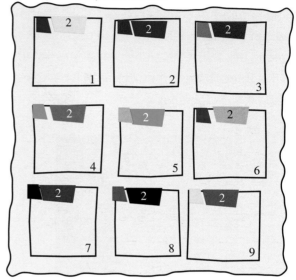

3. Begin with the game piece #3 of your first fabric. Place it on block #3, and repeat the sequential placement. This time, the last two fabrics (colors: orange and yellow) will be placed in block #1 and block #2.

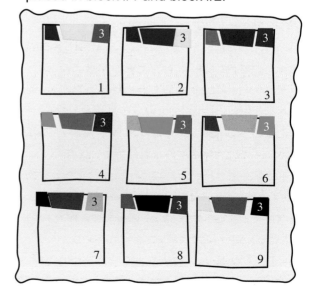

4. Repeat this process, placing fabrics sequentially until you have completed all nine blocks. The Wild Card fabric has not been used.

Round two . . . orderly disorder

At this point, your game board is very orderly. Now you will add some excitement to your quilt with some disorderly game-piece adjustments.

1. Before you sew, assess what you see. Should some game pieces be replaced with game pieces from different fabrics? Do you see a way to improve on the groupings? What would happen if you used just one or two of your Wild Cards? Give yourself permission to substitute an entire set of game pieces or, just one or two individual pieces. (Remember, you still have your template and six discarded selected fabric squares.)

2. Feel free to use even more fabrics than you originally selected. Sometimes just one strange fabric makes all the difference to make your piece become quite beautiful.

3. When you've assessed and are happy with what you see, then begin stitching one block

at a time until all nine blocks have been sewn. Please use a seam allowance of ⅛" rather than a normal ¼". With a narrower seam allowance, the alignment will be better. Keep in mind that nothing will totally match when each block is sewn together. Do not be concerned about perfect seam alignment.

4. If your fabrics don't align because of slippage that occurred as the fabrics were rotary cut, split the difference when you sew. Some pieces will be longer and some may be shorter, so find the center point of each of the pieces and go from there.

5. Square your blocks. Then create more disorder by arranging the blocks any way that pleases you. In other words, you don't have to keep the blocks in the same order that you created them on the game board.

Colorway Options

• Choose one color range. For example, choose generic reds. Then select 16 different reds. Generic reds may include colors from a dark ruby to true apple red, and a few orange reds, fuchsias, pinks, and grapes.

• Choose several scales. By using different types of fabric the game changes immensely.

• Choose neutrals in a variety of scales of grays, beiges, and browns. For this colorway, your Wild Card might be a crisp, black-and-white fabric.

Musical Chairs Quilts

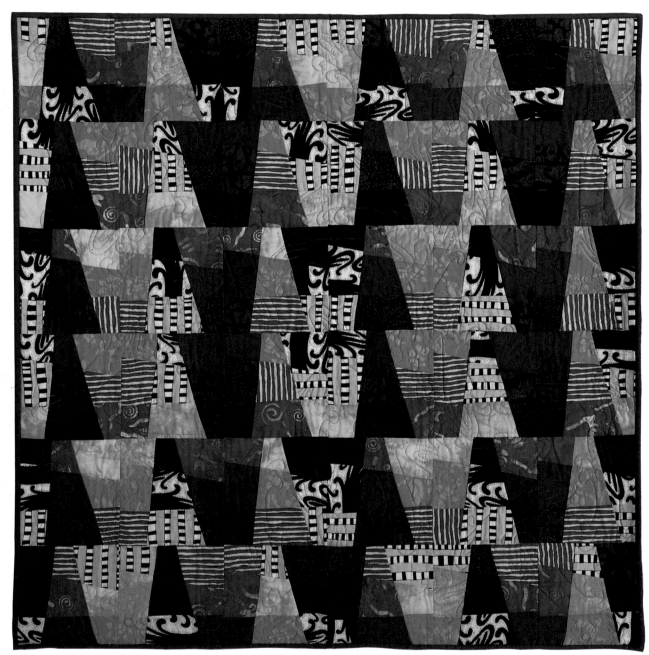

AFRICAN 9-PATCH
37" x 37"
Made by Berri Kramer, Kennebunkport, Maine.
Berri combined almost-solid fabrics with strong prints, stripes, and geometrics and
added another element of design by selecting a strong contrast in color.

The Missing Birthday Presents

38½" x 31½"

Made by Peggy Ireland Elliott, Cumberland, Maine.
By creating thin center game pieces, Peggy made her blocks
appear to have vertical and horizontal sashing that look like
ribbons wrapped around her gift boxes.

Out of Africa

47" x 31"

Made by Marcia Gibbons, Kittery Point, Maine.
Imagine how the piece perked up when Marcia added the five
black-and-white squiggly prints to her Musical Chair neutral palette.

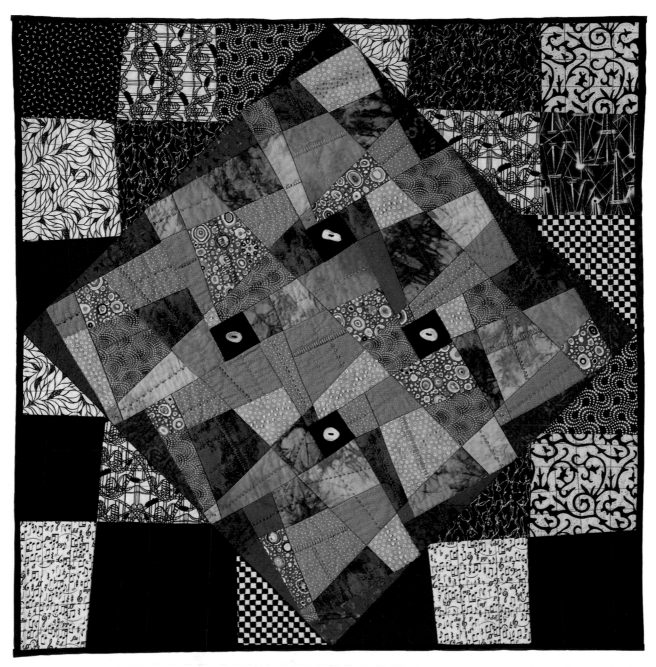

BARE BONES
33¼" x 33¼"
Made by Alice Hobbs Parsons, Belmont, Maine.
Alice set her blocks on point, then inserted a black fabric
that she embellished with real animal bones.

SALSA

43½" x 55½"

Made by Connie K. Carrington, Huntsville, Alabama.

Connie randomly sashed with a chartreuse red-pepper motif fabric and rearranged her blocks to achieve a staggered effect for her playing of Musical Chairs. Although created in a straight set, her quilt gives an impression of both order and disorder. Photo by Connie K. Carrington.

LITTLE CHAIRS

12" x 12½"

Made by the author.

Dianne achieved an illusion of motion in this little game of Musical Chairs.
She then embroidered French knots for added texture.

KITE CARTOONS
88" x 100"
Made by the author.
Dianne used Piano Keyboard to connect the upper and lower midpoint
sections of this quilt and for the top and bottom inner borders.

Piano Keyboard

Object of the Game

If you enjoy using geometric patterns in your quilts, Piano Keyboard will appeal to you.

The object of the game is to quickly make a random semblance of a piano's keyboard for use as a border or for inserting a "spacer" between design components or blocks. I find that with improv quiltmaking, I often end up with areas that need lengths of fabrics added, and Piano Keyboard serves that purpose nicely.

To see a perfect example of finding myself in such a design dilemma, look at the midpoint of KITE CARTOONS. The two sections adjacent to the "box kite" were in dire need of a connector fabric. I chose the game Piano Keyboard not only to serve as a space filler between the two areas, but also because Piano Keyboard carries a viewer's eye horizontally across the vertical sky and ribbons in the quilt.

Game Plan

I recommend a black-and-white colorway. For most improv quilts, these two solids usually work best because of the clarity of two sharply contrasting colors. Other solid colors also work well, depending on your piece. Select prints that read as solids if you have a real aversion to solids. For now, I will assume that you will be using black and white solids. Mock up your keyboard *after* play begins.

Your Move!

The moves are easy, and I know you will enjoy this game.

1. First, prepare your strips by cutting one 6" x 18" strip of each fabric: one black and one white.
2. Layer one on top of the other and place the two layers horizontally. Rotary cut wedge-shaped strips at random angles. Create gentle angles, all similar but not the same. Make the wedges not too wide and not too skinny.

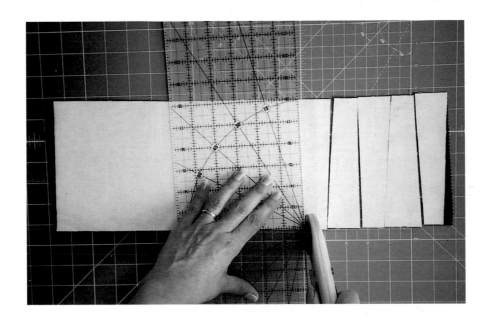

3. Create a mock-up by alternating one black with one white fabric. The way you lay out your pieces will determine how curvy or straight your keyboard becomes.

4. To create a curve, place the wider ends of the wedges side by side until you have accomplished a desired curve. To change the curve's direction, reverse this process by flipping the wider ends of the wedges to the other side. Continue in this way, manipulating the shape of the curve, until you have the desired look.

Wide ends
of wedges

Wide ends
of wedges

5. To get a straighter curve, alternate the wider ends more often.

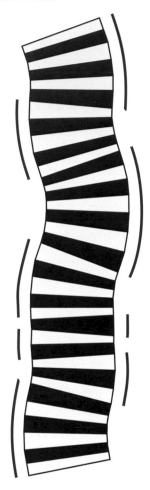

6. Your curve manipulation is important. It is possible to make two units from one keyboard but not if your keyboard is too curvy. If you want to cut two units, arrange the curves with a gentle concave and convex motion. Then, you will be able to cut a straight line through the middle of the keyboard, end-to-end, yielding two units. This is a time-saving advantage because you end up with two units by creating only one Piano Keyboard.

7. After your mock-up is complete, sew together all the units in order, alternating the two colors.

Attaching your Piano Keyboard to a quilt top

1. If you cut the border in the middle for two units, one side will be curved and the other straight. Attach the straight side to the quilt, keeping the curvy side as the exterior edge and bind with bias binding. Conversely, if you want the exterior edge to be straight, attach the curve to your quilt by piecing or by appliqué.

2. If you keep both sides curvy, it is easy to sew the curved unit. My trick is to hand appliqué the curves with a loose blind-stitch, then open up the seam to the inside. With my machine, I stitch over the seam line created by the appliqué with a normal running stitch. The first stitching (hand appliqué) acts as a basting stitch that may be followed to get an accurate machine stitched curve.

If you plan to use the entire border as one unit, you may want to manipulate the curves more strongly. The dotted line in the figure below shows that strong curves cannot make two units.

With this motion in your borders, I hope all your quilts sing with beautiful keyboard notes!

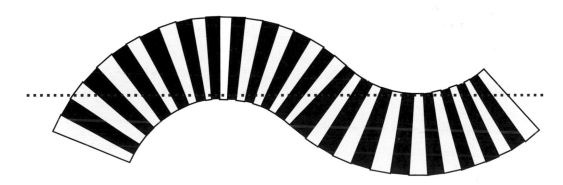

This keyboard is too curvy to cut into two separate units.

FANDANGO

29" x 26½"

Made by Linda Rogers, Monson, Massachusetts.

Linda's quilt is a great example of two games in one—
Checker-Border and Musical Chairs, arranged asymetrically.

Quilters Playtime - Dianne S. Hire

Checker-Border

Object of the Game

Geometrics, such as checks, especially in basic black and white, give sparkle and zest to a quilt in a way that no other color combination can. Sometimes the random nature of improv quiltmaking, with its combination of many fabrics, needs to be calmed down. The game Checker-Border, a random checked design, acts as this type of stabilizer. It's fun, it's easy to accomplish, and when you play, you create classy quilt borders or interiors. An irregular checkering adds whimsy to a quilt and keeps a quilt from being too serious.

I spoke with another quiltmaker, Polly White-horn of Great Neck, New York, about an article she wrote for the Spring 1999 issue of the *American Quilter* magazine. She constructs a two-fabric border similar to mine. We agreed that there's nothing new under the sun, but I want to give her credit for the publication of a similar method. I include my version here.

By now you've come to realize that I truly do have a childlike love of play. Join me, and let's play Checker-Border.

Game Plan

You can play Checker-Border in several ways. The easiest option is to play with two checker rows in black and white. Others, somewhat more complicated, are a Checker-Border with two rows with three or more fabrics, three rows with three or more fabrics, or a combination of these.

Detail from MUSICAL CHAIRS shows a border with two checker rows (full quilt pictured on page 78).

Detail from left side of KITE CARTOONS shows three checker rows with three fabrics (full quilt pictured on page 68).

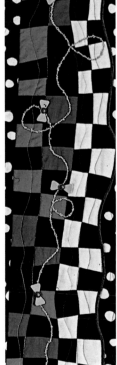

Detail from right side of KITE CARTOONS shows four checker rows (full quilt pictured on page 68).

Another way to play Checker-Border is to cut individual pieces and stitch them with alternating lights and darks.

Detail from left side of ORANGE AIR shows checker rows of multiple fabrics cut individually (full quilt pictured on page 77).

Colorways

Start with ½ yard of white and ½ yard of black. I use solid black and white fabrics for this game.

Feel free to substitute colors. If you use prints, let them read as solids. You will do a mock-up of your Checker-Border *after* you start the game.

Your Move!
Cutting wedges for two rows

1. Fold two fabrics separately so you can cut four identical wedges from each fabric at one time.
2. Using your rotary cutter and ruler, cut out four white wedge-shaped units. Then cut four black wedge-shaped units. The white wedge shapes should be slightly different when compared to the black wedge shapes. If you like, you may cut the wedges separately so they are all different sizes.

Checker-Border Wedges

• Length: approximately 18" long (the length of ½ yard of fabric)

• Width: Varies from about 1½" to 2" at the narrow end to 2½" to 3½" at wider end. If you make wedges smaller than this, you will create a very narrow border–again, that is your choice. Later, when you are more comfortable creating this type of random border, widths may be manipulated easily.

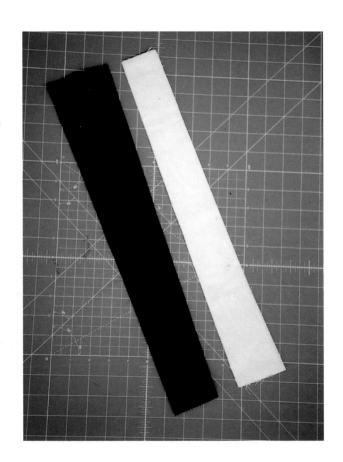

Sewing wedges

1. Stitch one white wedge to one black wedge. Always match a wider end to a narrow end to create one two-color unit.

2. Repeat stitching the remaining fabrics together into a two-color unit. You should have four of these units.

3. Press all four two-color units. Press the seam allowance away from the lighter of the two fabrics.

Cutting mini-wedges

1. Stack all four of the sewn units, alternating the units in the stack. A black unit will have a white one behind it and vice versa. This is done so that the mini-wedges differ when cut.

2. Cut gently angled wedges similar to the dotted lines marked in the figure below. Note that each angle is slightly different. As always, try not to cut parallel lines. Keep the cuts wedge-shaped. Vary the angles, but cut

nothing really sharp. I try to cut different widths with nothing less than 1½" or more than 2½". Sizes may be manipulated according to your quilt's needs. When you cut the mini-wedges, keep in mind the overall width of your Checker-Border. You don't want to make it too narrow.

3. When you finish cutting, leave the black-and-white mini-wedges randomly stacked, just as you cut them.

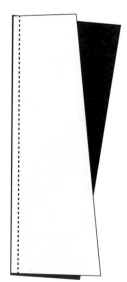

Match the wider end to the narrow end.

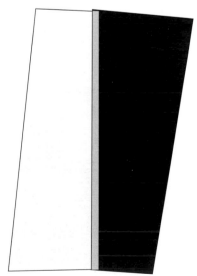

Press the seam allowance toward the darker fabric.

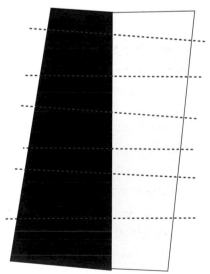

Cut mini-wedges at gentle angles.

Mock-up your Checker-Border

1. Pick up mini-wedges from different stacks that are not next to each other. Alternate the colors to get the checkerboard pattern. Allow soft, flowing movement as you assemble the mini-wedges, readying for sewing. Do not necessarily match the points. Sometimes match them and sometimes don't match them. Let the flow tell you how to arrange the curve to make motion.

2. To get a curve, place your units together with several wider ends at the top, then reverse this to change the curve. This is the same curve method as in Piano Keyboard (page 70).

Sewing mini-wedges

1. Stitch the mini-wedges together, keeping the order of your mock-up intact.

2. As you sew your mini-wedges together, you may need to add a mini-wedge to your mock-up to fit a specific place in order to curve correctly.

Playing with three checker rows

1. The game may be made more intricate by using a variety of different fabrics. Although you keep an overall effect of alternating lights with darks, more visual movement can be achieved by varying colors, scales, and designs. The result is a Checker-Border illusion.

2. For three rows with only two colors, rotary cut three 18" wedges of each of your two fabrics. Sew three wedges together, alternating colors black, white, black. Sew three more together. This time alternate white, black, white. Rotary cut mini-wedges just like you did previously.

3. Do a mock-up, alternating colors. Stitch the three-part mini-wedges together, and press.

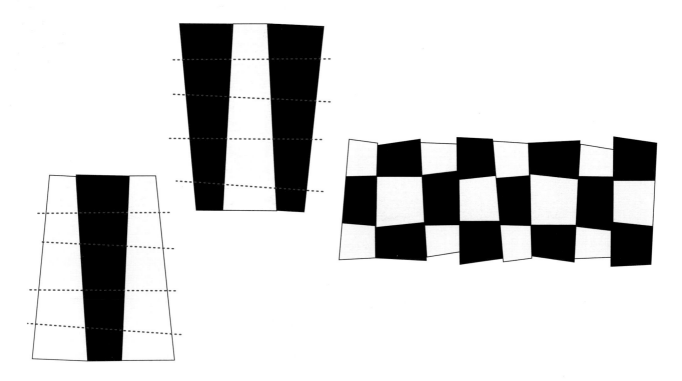

Checker-Border Quilts

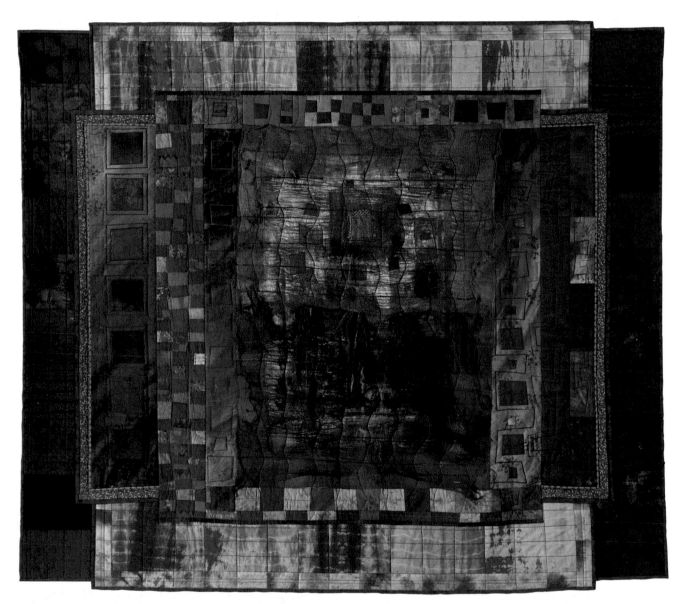

ORANGE AIR
79¾" x 71"
Made by the author.
Dianne's medley of games and techniques includes multicolored
Checker-Borders with alternating lights and darks.

MUSICAL CHAIRS
54¼" x 53¼"
Made by the author.
Dianne's Checker-Border echoes the black-and-whites she used throughout her quilt.

SOFT MUSICAL CHAIRS

28½" x 36"

Made by Carolyn Ingram, Huntsville, Alabama.

Muted hand-dyed fabrics gently blend into a stunning Musical Chair block
arrangement that is sharpened with her Checker-Border at the bottom edge.

STARS IN THE OUTBACK

52" x 66"

Pieced by Glenola Bush, Alameda, California, and quilted by Kathy Sandbach.

Glenola added a straight-cut blue-and-black Checker-Border to her sampler of game blocks.

Brave New World 911

46" x 33"

Made by Berri Kramer, Kennebunkport, Maine.

Berri created this quilt to commemorate the 2001 loss of the New York World Trade Center twin towers. I saved this incredibly beautiful quilt until the end of this game. Her quilt is a combination of several *Playtime* games, albeit mainly an array of Checker-Borders. Look carefully to find Hopscotch, Piano Keyboard, and her version of Tic-Tac-Toe with inserts. Berri's use of black and white with very little other color creates a strong design impact.

GLINT

22" x 26¾"

Made by Sally K. Field, Hampden, Maine.

The navy backdrop and multi-orange sticks make this quilt glimmer with elegance.

Sally chose shimmery fabrics and glitzy lamés for sparkle and shine.

Pick-Up-Sticks

Object of the Game

The object of the game of Pick-Up-Sticks is to create multiple paper-pieced strips of sticks and backgrounds. Assemble the strips into a wallhanging with normal quilt binding, or use the strips as a border for a larger quilt. Both are good ways to play the game.

Game Plan

To accomplish that goal, the first strategy is to select a colorway. In preparation for play, consider what you want for a finished product. Color changes the character or the nature of a quilt. As you can see from the three quilts by quiltmakers Sally K. Field (GLINT, pictured on page 82), Alice Hobbs Parsons (MOM'S VISIT, pictured on page 86), and Peggy Ireland Elliott (CANDY, pictured on page 85), immense diversity from the same instructions is achieved simply by varying the colorway.

One colorway that keeps coming to mind is classic black and white. Think about how elegant a white ground with crisp black sticks might look. "Black" may be interpreted by introducing other dark colors: shades of brown, navy, purple, green, and gray. All of these add interest and life to black. Additionally, if different textures, such as shiny lamé-type fabrics, are used, imagine the beauty of the Pick-Up-Sticks quilt. In the same way, white has more visual effect, depth, and movement when more than one white is used. Equally, a quilt created in the exact opposite colorway (black ground with white sticks) would be pure sophistication. A

segment of each of these colorations into one piece might be breathtaking.

To play Pick-Up-Sticks, gather these supplies: a pencil, some graph paper, a ruler, paper scissors, fabric shears, and a sewing machine with a sharp needle and be ready to play.

Your Move!

The following moves assume that you are familiar with paper piecing. Although there is an element of free-form intuition, it is easiest to create the basic strip-pieced row by using your favorite paper-piecing technique. Have fun, and enjoy playing Pick-Up-Sticks.

Round one... drawing strips

1. Draw 10 rectangular strips on graph paper, with the following dimensions: (If you are using 8½" x 11" graph paper, you will need to tape two sheets end to end to get your 20" lengths. You will need four of these taped-together sheets.)

   - 3 strips 20" x 2½"
   - 2 strips 20" x 2"
   - 3 strips 20" x 3"
   - 2 strips 20" x 4"

   These dimensions will make a 20" x 27" finished piece. If you want to change any of these measurements, go for it. It is your piece, and I encourage your creative input.
2. With paper-cutting scissors, cut the 10 rectangular strips of graph paper.
3. With your ruler, randomly draw wedge-shaped sticks on the graph paper rectangles. Draw the lines at different angles—gentle, of

course—in different widths (none very fat and none very skinny), and in different directions. Do not, however, intersect or overlap them. Allow space between each one and vary the spaces. The idea is to see more background than sticks when the pieced strip is finished.

Randomly draw wedge-shaped sticks on graph paper ready for paper piecing.

Round two...
cutting sticks and background

1. To get started, cut various background fabrics as follows:
   • 5 different fabrics, 3" x 6"
   • 5 different fabrics, 3½" x 6"
   • 5 different fabrics, 4" x 6"

• Cut additional background pieces as needed.

2. For the sticks, cut various fabrics as follows:
   • 5 different fabrics, 3" x 4"
   • 5 different fabrics, 3½" x 4"
   • 5 different fabrics, 4" x 4"
   • Cut additional pieces for sticks as needed.

Round three... piecing strips

1. Use your favorite paper-piecing method to sew your sticks and backgrounds. Vary backgrounds—sometimes use several of the same fabrics and colors in a sequence and sometimes transition to others. In the same way, vary the sticks. Perfect grain lines are unimportant.

2. Assemble your pieced strips to make a quilt top. To use this game for a border, draw a graph paper design that is a length and width appropriate for your quilt.

Hints

• Although it is true in paper piecing that whatever you draw will be reversed when sewn, because of the improv nature of this game, it makes no difference at all. When you draw sticks on the next graph paper row, do not be concerned about matching any lines for the sticks or background. Draw randomly.

• Quiltmaker Sally K. Field suggests that you work without cutting numerous fabric strips in advance. Instead, address one 20" strip of graph paper at a time. Measure the longest individual drawn line, whether it is a stick or a stick background. That measurement should be your barometer for the longest length needed.

Pick-Up-Sticks Quilts

CANDY
17" x 20"
Made by Peggy Ireland Elliot, Cumberland, Maine.
Peggy used a neutral background with wider slivers of colored sticks.
To achieve the effect of alternating a dark and light, Peggy added an overlay
of netting, heavy quilting, and happy colored fabric "buttons."

MOM'S VISIT

20" x 27½"

Made by Alice Hobbs Parsons, Belmont, Maine.

Alice's quilt shows how simple gradations can be used in both
background and the dominant vertical sticks for a beautiful quilt.

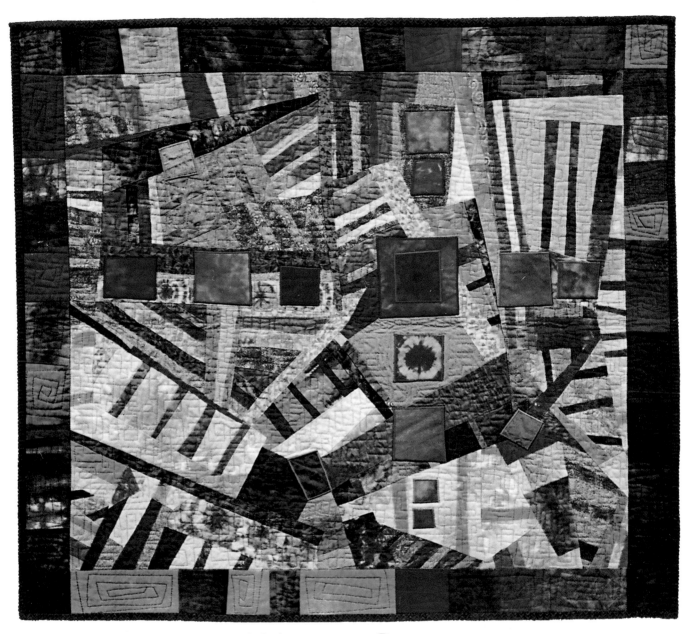

WHACKY-STIX

35" x 31¾"

Pieced by the author and quilted by Nancy R. Board.
Dianne created several 4" to 5" squares of the paper-pieced sticks. Then she
rotary cut the squares into random pieces and sewed them back together.

No one knows what may come out of this array of fabrics. Hints may get distorted according to your own interpretation of generic instructions.

Puzzler

Object of the Game

Puzzler puts deductive reasoning to the test. The object of the game is to create a block or a complete quilt from written hints. Pretend someone is softly whispering general instructions for making the finished piece into your ear.

Ordinarily, I am puzzled about the direction a quilt will take when I spontaneously start a new quilt. I often begin in a very similar way as in the game Puzzler. By practicing and playing the game, you will become comfortable in creating your own spontaneous designs.

On purpose, I give only generic instructions as to how to proceed with play.

Game Plan

To plot out your strategy, you must go straight to making your moves. Why? When you play this game, you are on your own as you respond only to written hints.

Several complete quilts have been created by quiltmakers who used the game instructions. Those quilts are shown on the following pages, but please do not turn to them until you have played the game yourself. You will find it fun to compare your Puzzler interpretation with how each quiltmaker heard the same instructions.

The beauty of this game is that no quiltmaker has created anything similar to another's piece.

Your Move!

Remember, these words are written so that you may interpret them in several ways. It is the receiver of the hints who uses the words and reads between the lines to come up with a unique and fun quilt.

Rules of the game

1. Take two pieces of fabric, oh, say, around 6" x 3".

2. Sew them together, pinning if need be.

3. Cut them apart a couple of times.

4. Flip one piece around.

5. Resew all of the pieces together, forming a "block."

6. Repeat and create more blocks.

7. With a rotary cutter, adjust the block size to whatever you like or need.

8. Sew these together and see what you get.

9. You have permission to add borders, sashing, and other things, as long as your block can be ascertained after you've played.

Please, do not turn the page until you have played this game!

The origination of PUZZLER was the result of telephone instructions given to Sally K. Field, who had enrolled in one of my workshops. Sally called, wanting to start playing several days before the class was to begin. I quickly made up some directions over the phone. Here are the photographs of her piece in progress and the completed quilt, which was based on the directions she heard me give.

Cut them apart a couple of times.

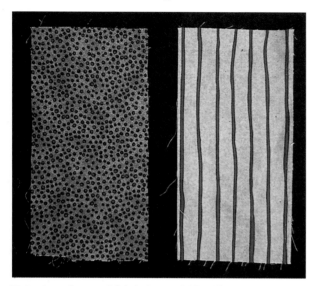

Take two pieces of fabric around 6" x 3".

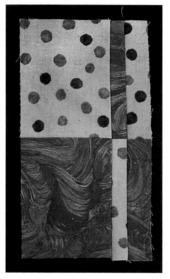

Flip one piece around. Resew all of the pieces together, forming a "block."

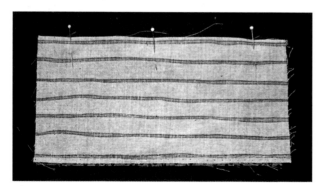

Sew them together, pinning if need be.

Repeat and create more blocks. With a rotary cutter, adjust size to whatever size you like or need. Sew together. (Follow the instructions on page 89.)

Evolution of a Puzzler quilt

Watch as Alice Parsons begins with a simple piece with dangling tails from Pin the Tail on the Donkey. In Alice's first Puzzler version, it is already a lovely example of the Puzzler block.

Dissatisfied with the first attempt, in her second version, Alice took apart the top two Puzzler blocks and inserted a third one. By adding the gray borders, the quilt took on an oriental flavor, with its kimono shape.

First version of Alice's Puzzler play

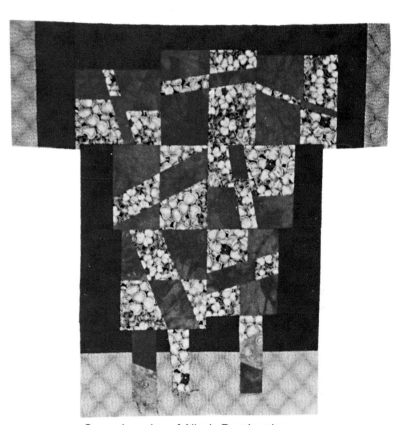

Second version of Alice's Puzzler play

For the final version of her Puzzler quilt, Alice turned her second version on its side, attached tails, antique buttons from her grandmother Lula, and ceremonial Chinese necklace beads (ca. 1912) from her aunt Rosalee. Then she added yet another skewed blue background, and all of that sits on hand-quilted dupioni silk. She named her quilt LULA AND ROSALEE in honor of these special ladies.

LULA AND ROSALEE
25¼" x 28¼"
Made by Alice Hobbs Parsons, Belmont, Maine.
This is Alice's final version of her Puzzler play. Alice Parsons took her Puzzler
quilt through several transformations before arriving at this magnificent version.

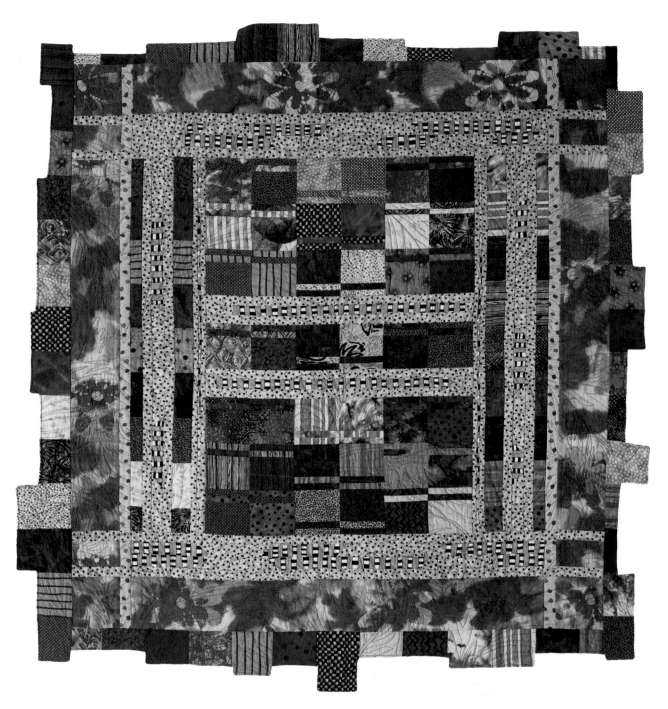

GOSSIP IN THE GARDEN
46½" x 50¾"
Made by Sally K. Field, Hampden, Maine.
Sally followed the Puzzler hints in a straightforward way. With her completed quilt, Sally
was adamant that it was a love/hate relationship. She faced all those difficult, uneven
edges with love. She also said, "I love the finished look of GOSSIP IN THE GARDEN."

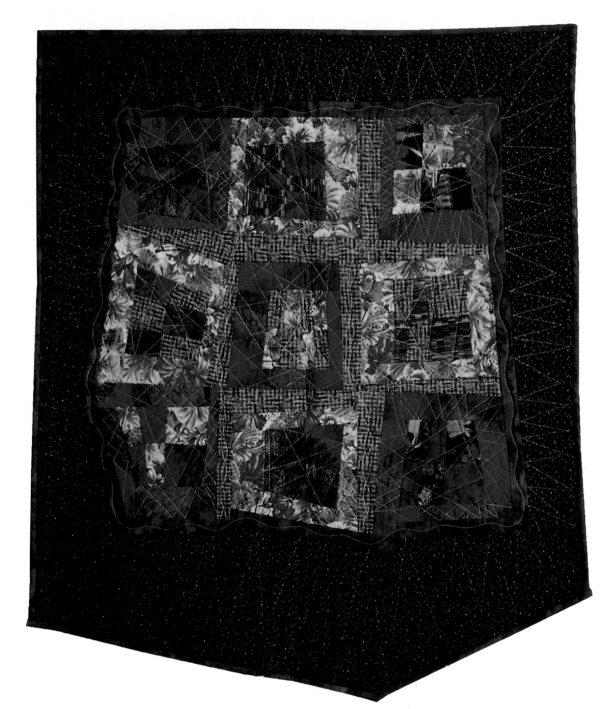

GOLLYWOMPERS 9-PATCH

31½" x 38"

Made by Judi H. Bastion, Augusta, Maine.

Judi stitched pairs of 6" x 3" fabrics together vertically and sliced the
units apart at various angles. She randomly switched and flipped
different fabrics and added borders to unify the design.

FIELDS OF GOLD

15½" x 18"

Made by Nancy R. Board, Amherst, Massachusetts.
Nancy read the clues and created this small quilt. She combined gold-toned fabrics in
cottons, silks, and poly-mixes into the same-shaped block, turned each in a different direction,
and then inserted a slender purple strip to break up the gold colors for a delightful quilt.

11/10-8

Made by Alice Hobbs Parsons, Belmont, Maine.
Alice's first interpretation of the Puzzler instructions
became a kimono shape. It was cut apart before being
measured and became "Buttoned Down."

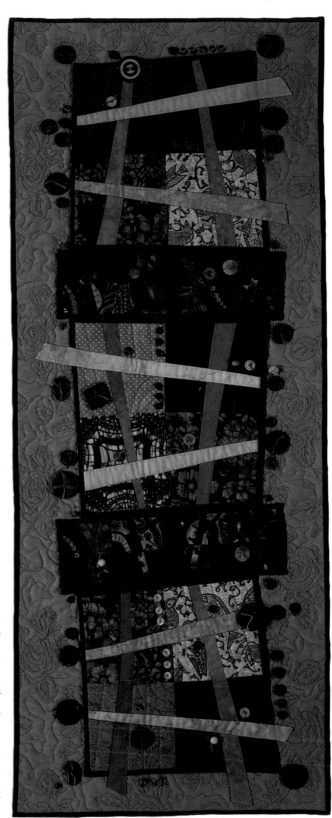

BUTTONED DOWN

22½" x 57½"

Made by Alice Hobbs Parsons,
Belmont, Maine.

In this interpretation of the Puzzler
instructions, Alice reconfigured a vertically
layered quilt onto a textured upholstery fabric.
Over 100 buttons of many colors and sizes are
hand sewn onto the quilt. Her Puzzler game
is shown as the two dark units that connect
three Tic-Tac-Toe blocks.

Clowning Around
27" x 36"

Made by Peggy Ireland Elliott, Cumberland, Maine.
Peggy created a fabric combination that just makes us laugh as if
she is winking at us. Her concentric uncircles are all the same size,
but turning them in various directions makes them appear to be different.

Tiddly Winks

Object of the Game

When you think of the childhood game of Tiddly Winks, strewn luminous plastic disks come to mind, the arrangement falling in a wondrous assortment of overlapping colors. The goal of Tiddly Winks for quilts is to create blocks in multiple colors, while following rules for laying out fabric pieces sequentially. In general terms, Tiddly Winks is a game of fused concentric fabric "uncircles." The finished piece is a delightfully simple arrangement of circular color that only appears difficult to create.

Game Plan

There are two parts to your game plan. The first is what fabric choices you will make, and the second is how you will interpret the rules to complete the game.

If two different quiltmakers took the same chaotic handful of fabrics and restructured those disparate colors into the same design, the finished pieces would be similar but not the same. One of the truly exciting things about quiltmaking is that each of us arrives at a personal interpretation of shape and design, even when we begin with the same fabrics.

The game of Tiddly Winks offers the potential for such variety. With a handful of assorted fat quarters, any version of Tiddly Winks will produce a wonderful interpretation in quilt form. Playing does not require a huge amount of any one fabric for the blocks.

Colorways

Let's talk about the fabric choices. Tiddly Winks is excellent for just about any types of fabric.

The fabrics dance with great motion if strong, dynamic prints are used. On the other hand, there is an almost serene feeling of gentleness when hand-dyed fabrics, batiks, soft prints, or moderate geometrics are used. It works for both ends of the spectrum, from traditional fabrics to wild ethnics, from homespun plaids to fun children's prints. Tiddly Winks would probably work equally well for an assortment of calico prints and for several sizes of large florals. When prints are chosen, use a variety of scales to achieve a dimensional effect. You will need either nine or 12 fabrics for the game play.

Rules of the game

Because the piece develops step-by-step, completion decisions can be made during the game play. There are two versions of the game: Tiddly Winks, in which each block is kept intact, and Broken Tiddly Winks, for which the blocks are cut into segments and rearranged.

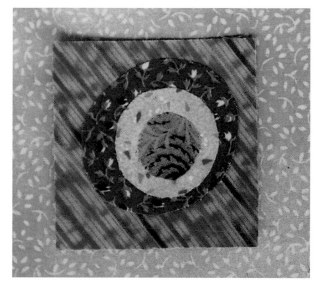

Tiddly Winks is played with blocks of concentric uncircles in multiple colors.

Broken Tiddly Winks is played with blocks that have been cut into segments then rearranged.

Your Move!

To prepare for play, in addition to basic quilt-making supplies, please gather the following items:

- transparent tape
- glue-stick
- paper scissors
- several sheets of plain white paper
- a few sheets of graph paper at least 10" x 10"
- a piece of thin cardboard at least 10" x 10"
- paper-backed fusible webbing (3½ yards)
- To create accurate circular cuts, you will need a small 28 mm rotary cutter with a new (very sharp) blade.

Round one . . .
making a Tiddly Winks template

Regardless of which Tiddly Winks game you decide to play, you begin the same way by making a template.

1. Draw a 10" x 10" square on your graph paper. Anything smaller or larger will make the block more difficult to create. (You may need to tape together two sheets of graph paper to get the 10" width.) Find the center point of your square and mark it with a dot. Set the graph paper aside.

2. On your plain paper, freehandedly draw several "uncircles" in a variety of sizes from about 3" across to 7" or 8" across. Make some of the shapes almost round, and make others more oval or egg-shaped. Keep the shapes smooth-edged and simple, almost circular.

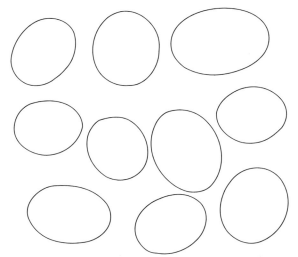

Draw a variety of uncircles, some almost round and some more oval.

3. Cut out several shapes that you like.
4. Do a mock-up of your paper shapes. Play with them until you find three different-sized shapes that work well when arranged concentrically inside the graph paper square. Leave a minimum space of ½" to ¾" around each shape. Don't use circles that are too large (little background may be seen) or too small (difficult to cut).

5. For a seam allowance, leave a minimum of ½" to ¾". Place the circles far enough away from the edge of the square to allow for the square's color to be seen as part of the overall design.

6. Once you are satisfied with the placement of the circles, trace around the selected three shapes with a sharp-pointed pencil onto the graph-paper square. Draw a straight line from the outside of the template to the center dot. This line will help you keep the circles aligned when you return them to the master template.

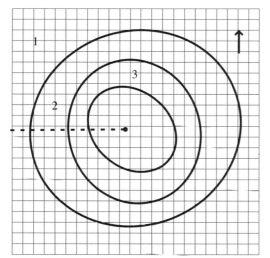

7. Mark an upward pointing arrow at the top of the square. This arrow is important and will help to keep everything going in the right direction later.

8. Number each part of the template as indicated in the figure above. Glue the graph-paper layout to the cardboard to create a master template. *Do not cut out* any of it just yet. Set aside the template for later use.

Round two ... selecting fabrics for play

For nine to 12 blocks, select 12 fabrics. Nine of the 12 fabrics should be separated into three darks, three mediums and three lights. The other three fabrics might be selected according to a specific color. As an example, for the fabric selection in the figure below, there are three neutral groups and a group of reds in medium tones.

Nine fabrics selected as darks, mediums, and lights, plus three fabrics in medium shades of red

Round three ... fabric stacking sequence

1. In preparation for rotary cutting, create three stacks of fabrics, right side up, as follows:

   Stack 1: Take one from each of four groups of fabrics in the order of one dark, one medium, one light, and one medium red.

   Stacks 2 and 3: For each stack, take one dark, one medium, one light, and one medium red.

   It makes no difference if the stack begins or ends with the dark fabric on top or on the bottom. Just be consistent with the above list for all four stacks.

2. Lay those three stacks of four fabrics one on top of the other, keeping the order of dark-medium-light-medium intact. You now have one stack of 12 fabrics.

3. From this one 12-fabric stack, create two stacks. Do not change the order of the fabrics. One stack will consist of the top six fabrics and the other stack will contain the last six fabrics.

4. Iron the stacks to compress them. This makes rotary cutting much easier.

Round four . . . cutting out your game pieces

This is important! Please read this entire section before cutting any fabric.

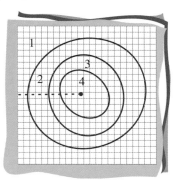

1. Begin by rotary cutting your stacked fabrics into squares the exact size of your template.

2. With paper scissors, cut along the dotted straight line of the template to the center dot as above. Then cut out around the circular line between shapes #1 and #2.

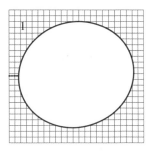

3. Using the outer square piece of the template (labeled #1), trace the circle on the top fabric of both fabric stacks (shown in white in the illustration below). Depending on which shows best on dark or light fabrics, use either a white marking pencil or a purple disappearing ink pen.

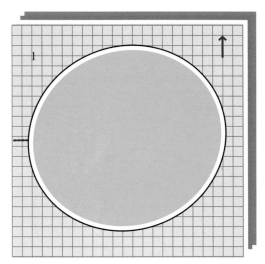

4. Remove the template and carefully rotary cut around the traced line through all six fabric layers. Leave the cut pieces in place.

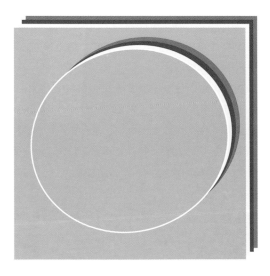

5. Repeat steps 3 and 4 for the second stack of six fabrics.

6. Replace piece #2 in your template by taping it on the back. Cut out piece #3. Trace around the inside of piece #2 on each fabric stack.

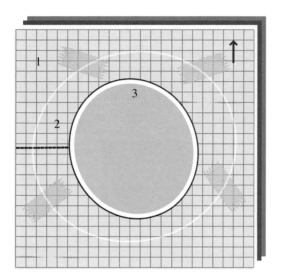

7. Remove the template and rotary cut around the traced line on both stacks of fabric. Again, leave the cut pieces in place.

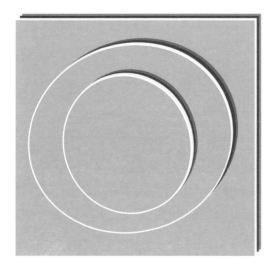

8. Tape piece #3 back into the template. Repeat the previous steps for cutting and tracing piece #4.

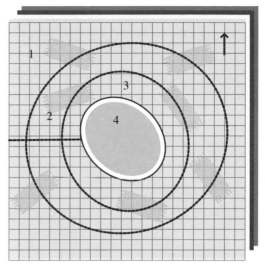

9. Repeat the rotary cutting of both stacks and replace piece #4 into the template.

Round five . . . Tiddly Winks mock-up

Ready to have some real fun? Now is the time to see your efforts pay off with incredible beauty and play. Not only is it a joy to see blocks begin to dance in colorful contrasting units, it's fun to lay them out on the wall as you do your mock-up.

Remember to keep your fabric pieces stacked in the original order that you decided on before you started cutting your game pieces. You will begin a mock-up of your Tiddly Winks blocks by laying out your exterior squares, shape #1, in a 3 x 3 grid or 3 x 4 grid, depending on whether you are doing a 9-block or a 12-block quilt.

1. Working from left to right and starting in the upper-left corner of your array, lay out all of game pieces #1 according to the original stacking order of the fabrics.

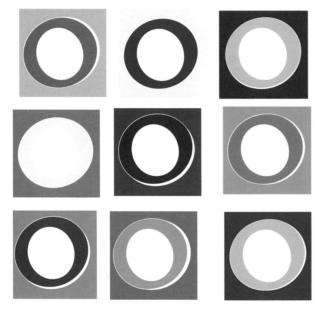

2. To lay out the #2 pieces, skip two blocks in the top row and begin the sequence of colors in the top-right corner. In the previous figure, look for piece #2 in light green in the upper-right corner block. Start with that piece and compare the stacked colors to the order in which the #2 pieces have been placed.

3. When you get to the end of the array and you still have some #2 pieces, go back to the beginning of the array in the top-left corner and keep going.

4. To begin the layout of piece #3, skip two blocks again and continue the sequential layout as before. If your colors work better by skipping only one block or more than two blocks for piece #3, try that. In the figure below, find the light-green piece #3 and compare the sequence of colors to the stacked colors.

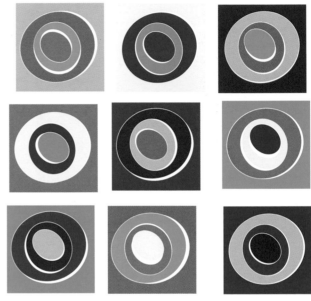

5. Repeat the same procedure for piece #4. Compare the color placement of the #4 pieces with the stacked colors in the previous figure.

6. When your mock-up is complete, assess your color combinations. Possibly search for a Wild Card (see pp. 17-18) if a fabric strikes you as not quite right. Use the *offending* circular shape as a template to selectively cut a replacement fabric.

Final round . . . fusing game pieces

1. Depending on the number of blocks you plan to create, cut nine or 12 pieces of lightweight paper-backed fusible webbing the same size as your template square.

Cutting Tiddly Winks

- Use a cutting mat that is large enough for your 10" block but small enough so that it can be rotated as you cut. A more accurate cut and a better circle will be accomplished if you rotate the cutting mat.

- Your goal is to create a smooth, continuous cut around each shape. As hard as you may try, however, there will probably be some "sliver-bloopers" and a few cases of

"gaposis". My pieces certainly did. The dreaded gaposis does not show on Cathy Cole's delightful quilt GAME BOARD, pictured below.

- Another way to cut out your shapes is to cut out all of your template cardboard pieces and trace all the lines at once. Then begin cutting with the *innermost* circle first. (Sally K. Field offers this tip.) She found that the fabrics were less wobbly and she had more fabric to hold with her fingers.

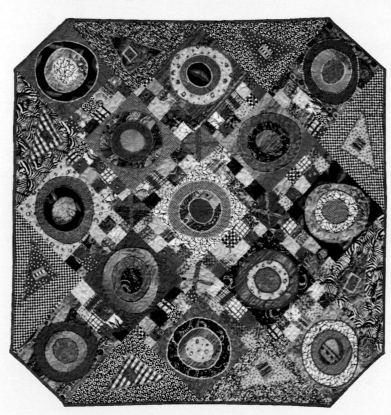

GAME BOARD

49" x 49"

Pieced by Cathy Cole, Windsor, Vermont, and quilted by Filament Formations. Cathy accomplished her sliver-blooper cover-up with delightful stitchery. By sashing and setting the Winks on point, her octagonally arranged array of prints is similar to a real game board.

2. Work on one block at a time. Carefully position the game pieces for a block on a piece of fusible webbing, with the fabrics wrong side against the webbing. Use your template as a reference if you inadvertently get pieces turned around.

3. At your ironing surface, check to see if all the shapes match and align to each other.

4. Place all the fabrics in the first block, adjusting the placements to get the fewest sliver-bloopers as possible.

5. Follow the manufacturer's instructions for thoroughly fusing your blocks together.

Decision time

It is now decision time. Do you want to play Broken Tiddly Winks? If not, remove the paper and fuse each block intact to a background fabric. If you prefer for that background to show as a border, cut your background larger. If you only want the block as you see it now, then iron it onto any fabric ground that does not shadow through to the front of the block. Add fancy stitchery embellishment or a fine satin-stitch appliqué. Then sash or simply sew the blocks together to complete the top.

Broken Tiddly Winks

1. If you want to play Broken Tiddly Winks, draw a template for cutting each block into four unevenly sized and shaped pieces.

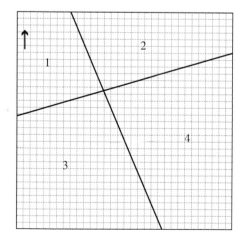

2. Remove the paper backing from the fusible webbing on the back of each block. By removing the slick paper, the blocks will gently adhere without being permanent. Do not *even think* of getting near an iron after you remove the paper backing or all your fabrics will "glue" together. That is definitely not a good thing.

3. Carefully stack all of your blocks into one or two stacks depending on how your rotary cutter best cuts. Make certain that you place all the blocks with the circles going in the same direction.

4. Keeping your template intact, rotary cut each stack of blocks, using the same folding technique as shown on page 59.

5. Mock up a new arrangement of broken blocks against the background pieces, mixing block segments. Then fuse the broken blocks to their backgrounds.

Tiddly Winks Quilts

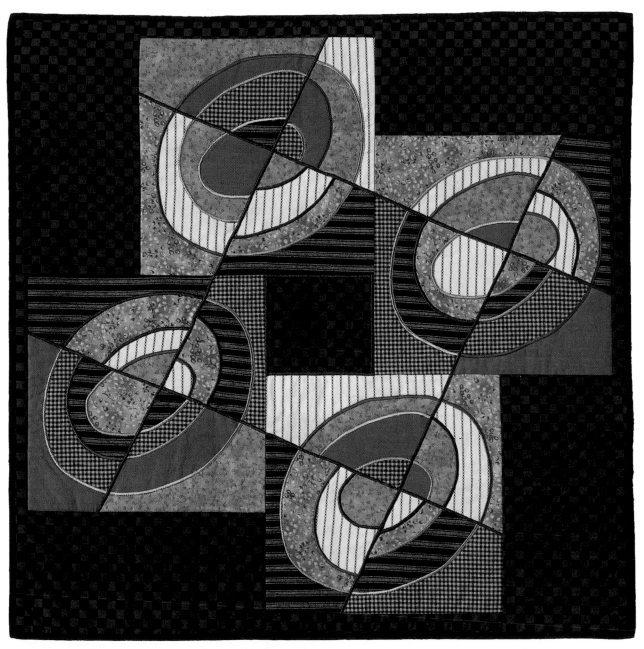

LOVING YOU
25" x 25"
By Alice Hobbs Parsons, Belmont, Maine.

Alice combined two different Tiddly Winks circular shapes in a flavor of the 1920's Art Deco
style. The gray-checked fabric reinforces that feeling in her colorway of pink, brown, and black.

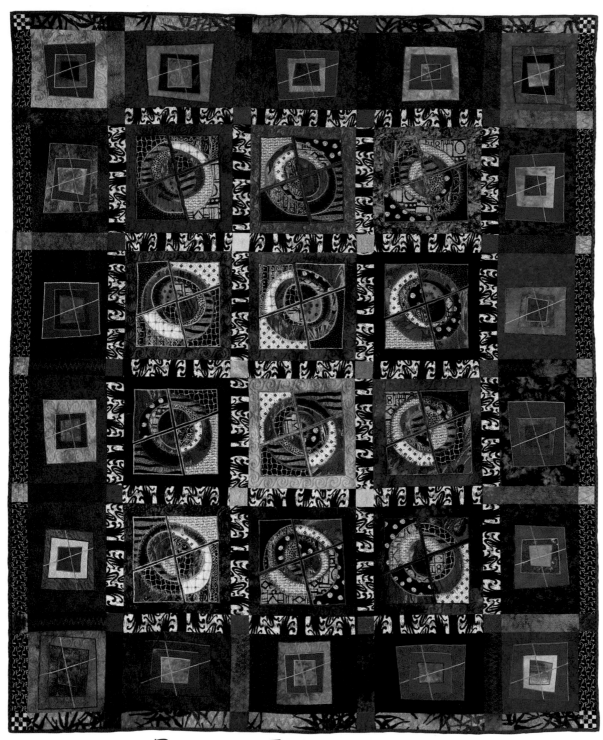

BROKEN TIDDLY WINKS

68" x 83"

Made by the author.

Dianne added a design element by fusing each of the 12 blocks onto
a larger background. All of the Wild Cards were selectively cut.

Come Upstairs
29" x 47½"

Made by Alice Hobbs Parsons, Belmont, Maine, and owned by Barbara and Galen
Plummer. Alice plays Broken Tiddly Winks. Instead of the winks turning in the same
direction, Alice gave her piece dramatic movement by changing a few blocks' orientation.

ROSY-ETTA STONES

38¾" x 55"

Made by the author.

To balance the weight of the large half-circular shaped area on
the right, Dianne created a medley of Rosy designs for this quilt.
ROSY-ETTA was happy to be chosen as *Playtime's* cover girl.

Ring Around the Rosy

Object of the Game

The goal of Ring Around the Rosy is to create circular designs called "rosies" that simulate flower petals. When completed, each Rosy is appliquéd, usually by machine, to a background.

Ring Around the Rosy was saved for last because it is slightly more advanced than earlier games. That shouldn't be a problem, especially if you have been playing along so far. By now, you "own" many of the techniques, and you understand intuitive piecing.

You can play Ring Around the Rosy as a "graduation" game, letting your creativity freely flow. You may proceed by merely looking at the photographs or actually trying out the suggestions laid out in the instructions. Either way, consider yourself a graduate.

Envision yourself adorned in a purple silk cap with a red sequined tassel and a chartreuse gown with orange polka-dot sneakers peeking from underneath, as you walk down a fabric-strewn aisle holding a hot pink vellum diploma wrapped in sparkling turquoise lamé. Congratulations!

Game Plan

Basically, make one easy change to the game of Hopscotch to play a simplified one-flower version of Ring Around the Rosy. In other words, a Rosy is made from a wedge-shaped version of a Courthouse Steps block with plain logs and pieced chimneys. "Stitching pairs" (described on page 115-116) is the key technique for sewing wedges into a circular shape. As with all of the *Playtime* games, there are no set rules of play and no specific design arrangements. The quilts are as unique as the players.

The strategy is to begin by making just one Rosy by using the now-familiar techniques of creating wedge-shaped pieces and using wallpaper cuts to match up dissimilar edges. As Alice Hobbs Parsons shows in her quilt REGALIA on page 118, one flower may develop into a single dominant image. On the other hand, many flowers can be used in an assortment of sizes as in ROSY-ETTA STONES on page 110.

In addition to fabric and the usual quilters' supplies, for this game you will need:

- 2 or 3 large (11" x 17") sheets of plain paper. (If you have only a smaller piece of paper, you can draw a half circle and rotate the half as you create a larger fabric unit.)
- a pencil and a string long enough to use as a compass

Colorways

Large-scale prints do not work as well as mottled tone-on-tone prints or hand-dyed fabrics. Scraps and fat quarters are excellent because small pieces offer a variety of each colorway, and that is what will make your Rosy sing.

For a Rosy, limit the colorways to two or three choices, depending on your design. For each colorway, find a number of similarly colored fabrics, gradations, or transitional fabrics. These can be fat quarters, scraps, or strips. Balance your selection for a varied Rosy and avoid selecting too many different prints and colorways without repeating any one. When you do that, your piece appears disjointed, fragmented, and is not nearly as appealing.

Rules of the game

Before you start sewing, build a mock-up by positioning fabrics around a circle drawn on paper. This drawn circle serves as a visual guide to create a flower shape as you encircle the axis with several different wedge-shaped pieces. In a Rosy, all of the wedges are narrower toward the center. The circular shape is achieved by rotating wedges around an axis, creating a shape that resembles a flower.

a.

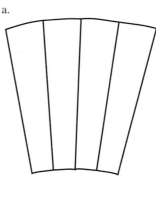

b.

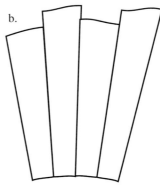

Rosies can have smooth or jagged outer edges.

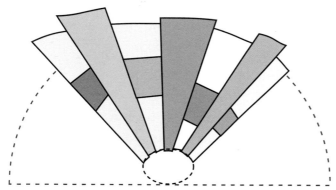

Alternate steeply wedged single fabric logs and pieced chimney blocks.

Notice that there will be a hole in the center, where there is no fabric sewn. That's the way it should be. The center of your flower will be the last fabric added to your Rosy.

Design choices

Rosies can have two kinds of outer edges. The outer edge will be almost smooth when all the wedges are the same length (as in the following figure a), or it will be jagged when the wedges are different lengths (b).

Many individual variations of Ring Around the Rosy may be created. As you play, let your imagination wander. Creating different permutations of a Rosy becomes almost compulsive, as you find new ways to sew them together and think of new, exciting color combinations to try. Here are some examples for ideas to get you started.

A simple Rosy has two colorways. Sewn pairs contain a solid fabric wedge and a pieced wedge in a chimney and log configuration similar to Hopscotch. Look at the result in the detail from ROSY-ETTA STONES on page 113.

With 2 colorways, alternate a pieced wedge with a single-fabric wedge.

Detail from ROSY-ETTA STONES (full quilt pictured on page 110). In this two-color Rosy, the petals are different fabrics in shades of reddish grape with unblocks of lemon lime.

A variation of this simple Rosy has two different sets of the flower petals with an interior and an exterior Rosy combined. Pairs of wedges make up the petals in each Rosy. Notice in the detail from ROSY-ETTA STONES that the outer yellow and blue pairs of wedges are half the width of the inner blue and red pairs.

Detail from ROSY-ETTA STONES. Yellowish prints are repeated in groups for outer petals.

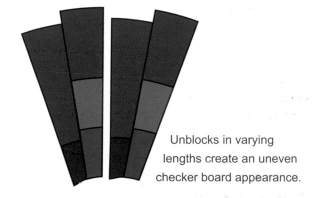

Unblocks in varying lengths create an uneven checker board appearance.

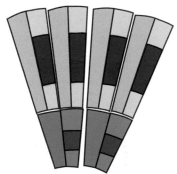

A variation of Rosy shows two colorways that combine interior and exterior portions of rosies.

Each pair of wedges can have three colorways. Varying the lengths of the unblocks in three colorways results in an uneven checkerboard effect as you can see in another detail from ROSY-ETTA STONES. All of the inner unblocks are cut from fabrics in the blue colorway.

Detail from ROSY-ETTA STONES (full quilt pictured on page 110). The third, bluish colorway creates interior petals.

Inserting a single-fabric wedge between pairs of wedges adds excitement and interest to another variation of a three-colorway Rosy.

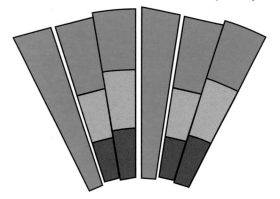

A single-fabric wedge can be inserted between pairs of three-colorway wedges.

Detail from ROSY-ETTA STONES (full quilt pictured on page 110). Wedges with three colorways interrupted by single-fabric wedges add to the effect of staggering the outer edges.

Your Move!

Your overall strategy is to create a mock-up from cut rectangles. You create wedges from the rectangles, trimming excess fabric here and there to stagger the unblocks in a checkerboard design and placing them back into your mock-up.

Mock-up

For a full Rosy, draw a complete circle. If you want to create less than a whole one, only draw the portion of the circle that you need (for example a half- or quarter-circle). For a small circle, use a compass, or in lieu of using a compass, attach one end of a string to a pencil and pin the opposite end to the center point on your plain paper. By changing the string's length, any size circle may be drawn.

This drawn circle serves as a visual guide to create a "mostly" circular shape as you sew. If you have only a small piece of paper, draw a half-circle and rotate it to create the larger mock-up.

Cutting and sewing wedges

The general instructions for how to create wedges in the illustration below can be used for sewing any Rosy. The dimensions are suggestions only. Feel free to vary your sizes as you like. A production method (stringing together the same task) works nicely. For a large Rosy, you may need up to 48 wedges in all; for a smaller Rosy, you may need as few as 30 wedges.

For ease in construction, your first Rosy should be fairly large, made with wedges anywhere from 10" to 15" long. Wedges can be 2½" to 4" across at the wide outer edge and ¼" to 1½" across at the narrow inner edge. The dimensions to the left make a Rosy about 10" long and 2½" wide, narrowing to about 1" at the inner edge.

Two different wedges are made from the same-sized rectangles.

1. Cut the following rectangles: For outer (red-violet) pieces of each wedge, cut a stack of rectangles 2½" by 4". For the center (red-orange) pieces cut rectangles 2½" by 3¼", and cut rectangles 2½" by 3" for the inner (blue) pieces. Cut 30 to 48 of each colorway.

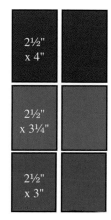

2. For the longer wedges, sew together some sets of the rectangles (about half of them) using a ⅛" seam allowance. Carefully press all seams in the same direction.

3. Cut wedges that taper to about 1" at the bottom. There is no need to measure; just eyeball a wedge shape. Cut all wedges approximately the same size without measuring. All flowers are unique just as your Rosy will be unique.

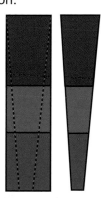

4. For the shorter wedges, start with the same set of rectangles and trim some excess off of the middle (red-orange) rectangles. Then join the pieces with a ⅛" seam allowance. Carefully press all the seam allowances in the same direction, then cut wedges the same way as you did in step #3.

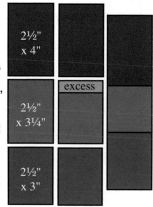

5. Replace each wedge onto your mock-up, using the paper circle as a guide. See how it is beginning to take a circular shape? All of your wedges may not fit onto your guide. That is because the wedges are presently larger than you need for a completed circle. It is time to make an artistic decision. Should you keep the size as it is for a much larger circle than you drew? Or should you rotary cut these into smaller wedges for a smaller circle? That is your choice.

Stitching pairs

1. For a staggered petal effect, align the first two wedges so that no seams match and sew them together as a pair. Repeat this process for the next pair of wedges and continue until all of your wedges are sewn as pairs, one to another.

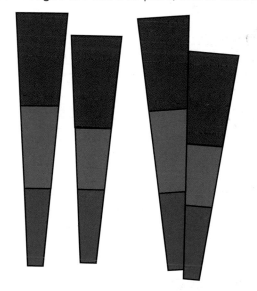

2. Lay sewn pairs onto to your drawn circle guide. Trim the sides of the wedges, without measuring, to fit into the mock-up. Repeat this process for additional pairs and continue to fill in the circular guide in your mock-up. Nothing

will be equal and the shape will not be a true circle. Remember, you are simulating flowers, and flowers are not shaped in perfect circles.

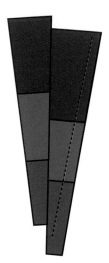

Trim sides as needed
to fit mock-up.

3. How do the trimmed pairs line up on your paper guide? Are they too large to go around the circle? Is the inner hole too large? Should they be smaller? Does everything lie flat? If not, perhaps shaving a little more off the wedge might work.

4. Rotary cut a bit from the inner portion of the wedge, leaving the outside as it is. Continue adjusting by alternately slicing a bit from one, then the other side of the pairs until a complete circle of fabric can be sewn together.

5. When everything fits nicely, sew all the pairs together. Then, if you find that you need more wedges, go back to the beginning instructions and create more wedges until your paper guide is completely filled in.

Fine-tuning around the Rosy

1. If you find there is still too much fabric and the circle has a bunching effect or that it doesn't lie flat, press out the bunching and resew some of the wedges. With the right side of the fabric facing you, carefully press one of the fabrics toward the seam so that it overlaps the seam and the actual seam disappears underneath the newly pressed area.

2. After you carefully press and all is flat, flip the Rosy to the wrong side and use the newly created pressing line as a stitching guide. Check to see if the fabrics fit better with this adjustment. If they do fit better, then cut off any extra fabric in the seam allowance rather than ripping out the first seam. Continue pressing and stitching until the Rosy is completely flat.

3. If you are new at eyeballing the angle of the wedges, here is a tip from Sally K. Field:

   Try joining pairs of wedges, then join the larger sections two by two. Continue enlarging sections in this way. It is easier to see where the inside of the wedge needs to be made smaller by rotary cutting.

4. The flower's center will be appliquéd last. Cover over the hole with a fused uncircle, and machine appliqué. If you wait until last to add the center, you will have great leeway in size manipulation and you may audition several centers.

Center Holes

• For a small hole, shorten the wedges at the center by about ½".

• For a medium hole, shorten the wedges at the center by about ¾".

• For a large hole, shorten the wedges at the center by about 1" to 1½".

Ring Around the Rosy Quilts

FIESTA

40" x 40"

Made by Sally K. Field, Hampden, Maine.

FIESTA sparkles with dynamic color and vibrates with floral movement, combining five different configurations of the game in overlapping bursts of reds and yellows, similar to Mexican dancers' skirts.

REGALIA

32" x 28"

Made by Alice Hobbs Parsons, Belmont, Maine, and owned by Rena Perley.
Alice incorporated bits of silk into the petals and embellished the 8" center with
olive-colored French knots and hand-embroidery for her powerfully distinctive quilt.

SQUASH BLOSSOM JOURNEY

20½" x 17½"

Made by Peggy Ireland Elliott, Cumberland, Maine.
Peggy created one dominant Rosy for this quilt, embellishing with
sparkly beads to honor her special friend, Lynn Collins.

Perceiver's Quilt A.K.A. "Everything is Colored by Black & White"

64½" x 65½"

Made by the author.

A circle within a square is the major design component. The black-and-white backgrounds create optical illusions of bold emerging/receding objects.

Toy Box

Every toy box has hidden treasures bumping around to play with. Here's your *Playtime* toy box with Marbles, Spinners, and Missing Pieces. Each of these toy-box treasures is fused instead of pieced. Just follow the instructions for fusing that are shown on your favorite type of fusing material.

Marbles

The goal of Marbles is to search for places where circles might be appropriately applied to a quilt's surface. Marbles are after-the-fact add-ons that can be appliquéd by machine or by hand. The detail from SALSA shows marbles rolling around along the border and in the center of the quilt top.

Detail from SALSA (full quilt pictured on page 66). You never know where something from your *Playtime* toy box might show up.

Marbles may also be the central focus of a quilt as in PERCEIVER'S QUILT A.K.A. "EVERYTHING IS COLORED BY BLACK & WHITE." Here the circle *is* the major design component and is the theme carried from the center to the border.

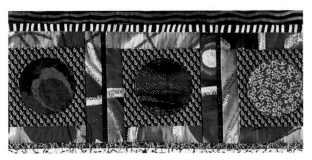

Detail from PERCEIVER'S QUILT A.K.A. "EVERYTHING IS COLORED BY BLACK & WHITE"

The game plan for Marbles is to locate fabrics that simulate the look of marbles, even though, in reality, they may not look at all like marbles. When you locate a fabric that you think may work as a marble, move a circular template over the fabric's surface to pinpoint the best areas.

Find the marble in the fabric.

Once I've found the perfect marble, I fuse it to my quilt surface, then finish its edges with machine appliqué. If you opt to apply these by hand, go for it!

A cat's-eye marble, whether in glass or fabric, is simply irresistible.

Quilters Playtime - Dianne S. Hire

Spinners

Remember those colorful plastic spiral spinners attached to a stick that you twirled around your body? When you think your quilt is almost finished, as always, assess its overall design. Does it still need something? Why not add a few whirling spinners?

Making spinners is easy and only requires a little practice. Do not be concerned if the spiral's widths are not even. In fact, if the widths are uneven as you go around the spiral, more design dimension is added.

To make a spinner, iron a piece of lightweight paper-backed fusible webbing to the back of your chosen fabric. Cut a rectangle about 6" x 10" so that several spirals can be made of the same fabric.

On the paper backing, draw several loose spirals with plenty of space to cut around. Spiral some from left to right, and some from right to left. Remember to keep the spirals loose. Tight spirals would be difficult to cut out and even

more difficult to go around with satin stitch machine appliqué. Also remember to leave at least ¼" to ⅛" of space on either side of the drawn spiral.

In your drawn spiral, be sure you leave enough space to work yourself into the center (blue dotted lines) and out of the spiral (red dotted lines). Find the black dot starting point in the figure below and with your finger, follow the blue dotted lines into the center of the spiral. Then follow the red dotted lines to the outside of it. That is how to cut your way into and then out of one pencil-drawn spiral. When you're done cutting you will have two spinners for the price of one!

Fuse your spinners in place and carefully machine appliqué them with a fine satin stitch around the spirals.

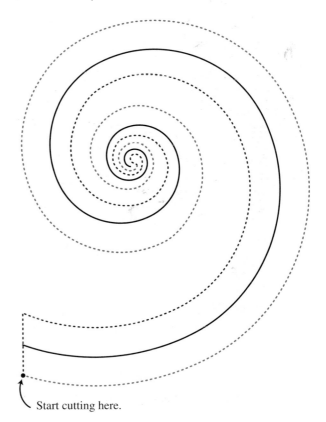

Draw a loose spiral with plenty of space to cut around.

Start cutting here.

AFTERGLOW

25" x 32"

Made by the author.

This was the first quilt Dianne made with spinners. If you squint and stare at this
quilt, then look away to a blank wall, you will see the spirals as an afterimage.

Missing Pieces

Finally, at the bottom of any toy box, you're bound to find some stray jigsaw-puzzle pieces that are missing from some completed picture. Your scrap basket may be full of such missing pieces. You may declare a quilt finished, but after hanging it on the wall, it may become obvious that something is missing in the overall design—like a jigsaw puzzle with a piece missing. At that point, sewn piecing may not be an option without a whole lot of fuss and trouble.

Here's a good motto: "When possible, find a way to keep from ripping out." So the solution is to add those missing design components by fusing fabric pieces onto the quilt's surface.

Basic to the strategy is an analysis of your piece. Ask yourself, "Do I need anything added to my quilt for it to stand up as good design?" If the response comes back as "Hmmm, it seems that something is missing," then consider fusing an additional component.

Pin a few fabrics here and there on your quilt, aligning them to other elements already in your quilt. Locate an area that appears to lack enough fabric information and place a few fabric pieces there. Don't be satisfied with the first trial. Take a break; leave the room; walk back in and quickly view the top. Often such quick viewing after a break will give great insight as to whether something more is needed. Or perhaps not!

The best way to see when an area has missing elements is to hang your quilt top on a wall rather than laying it flat on a table or floor. Your eye sees better that way. Use a viewing tool such as a reducing lens or, if you do not have that, try looking through an inverted end of binoculars. Both simplify anything you view, pinpointing and removing any extraneous information. Try it. It works.

Another way to see was learned from a gardener. Facing away from a section of her garden that she was considering renovating, she looked into a mirror that was directed at the garden. By viewing a mirror image, often you see design elements that may need to be revamped—just like in a garden. Try that, too.

Okay, there is another reason to add missing pieces to a quilt. Sometimes it is to cover up an element when there is something that is just not right. It may be something that does not align correctly, or the color may be wrong or lost on the surface. Yes, try a cover-up. Fuse a scrap over the offending element.

And with that, the *Playtime* games are concluded. My only advice: play your hunches, be impulsive, and find the fun. Thank you for playing along and just imagine that I am there with you, blowing bubbles to celebrate—and munching a chocolate bar.

Dianne

About the Author

Armed with a bachelor of arts degree in English and minors in French and philosophy, Dianne S. Hire rapidly changed her focus from language to fiber. Her 17-year career as a buyer of haute couture clothing introduced her to excellence in design and color. However, it was her grandmother Pearl Whitaker who introduced Dianne to the world of hand piecing when "Mammy" regained strength as she recovered from an almost fatal illness. From those beginnings as a traditional quiltmaker, it wasn't long before Dianne realized that she could combine her love of color, fabric, and design to create joyful and whimsical contemporary art quilts.

Soon, Dianne was asked to share her passion for fiber through lectures, then teaching. Quickly, she became a popular teacher whose students love her exciting and playful approaches to creating fiber art. Dianne's design games help her students develop their own sense of design, composition, and color usage while having tons of fun doing it. This book, a compilation of a few of those games plus others, is a furtherance of Dianne's enthusiasm for teaching and is her second book with the American Quilter's Society. Her early love of language returned when she edited and compiled *Oxymorons: Absurdly Logical Quilts!* as a joint project with The Renegades, an art quilt group from Maine.

In her spare time at home on the coast of Maine, Dianne creates what she calls her "summer piecing" as she designs and builds rock walls. With her husband, Terry, Dianne tends to their extensive gardens, which also reflect innovative design skills. She and Terry were adopted (and trained) by Sir Hilary Hire, a handsome Maine coon cat who happily shares his life with them.

Hurricane Barb Hits the Coast!

59" X 73"

Made by the author.

HURRICANE BARB was the first quilt Dianne made by using improv methods. It honors her special friend, Barbara, who creates spontaneous turbulence wherever she moves. Unpredictable and full of energy, she and the quilt are like a tightly wound low pressure in a hurricane.

Other AQS Books

This is only a small selection of the books available from the American Quilter's Society. AQS books are known worldwide for timely topics, clear writing, beautiful color photos, and accurate illustrations and patterns. The following books are available from your local bookseller, quilt shop, or public library.

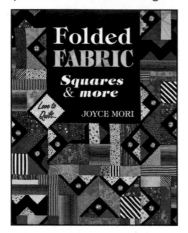

#6207   us$16.95

#6408   us$22.95

#5753   us$18.95

#6418   us$18.95

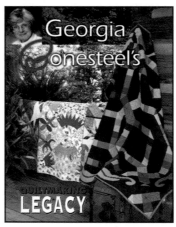

#6415   us$29.95

#6204   us$19.95

#6206   us$19.95

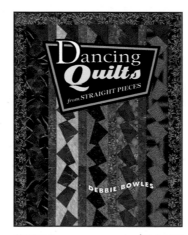

#6210   us$24.95

#5756   us$19.95

LOOK for these books nationally. CALL or VISIT our Web site at www.AQSquilt.com.

1-800-626-5420